Into the Wolf

Into the Wolf

what it takes to speak & be heard

SETH RIGOLETTI

ISBN: 979-8-9884182-1-4

Book design by Tom Morgan, Blue Design (www.bluedes.com)
Printed in the USA

Published by Salem Street Press
100 Commercial Street, Suite 405
Portland, ME 04101
www.sethrigoletti.com

TO MILO AND ELI

May you each trust your voice
and yourself, always.

CONTENTS

Foreword

started this book five years ago because I wanted to give my clients a supplemental tool to help them with their leadership communication skills. It has become so much more.

Over the years, I've worked with hundreds of clients who felt stymied in their professional life because of some behavior, belief, or habit that kept them from realizing their full potential. What became clearer after each session is that this "stuckness" was often more of an internal obstacle rather than an external one. I could see a trend happening between them all. These clients were exceptional at *what they did*. They were some of the smartest and thoughtful people I'd met, yet they were limited in the ways that they communicated their authority and their excellence to the rest of the world. They either struggled to have the courage to speak up, or when they did speak up, the message was unclear. Many were frustrated and uncertain whether change was possible. I knew that I could help them, if they were willing to be open.

All they needed was to get out of their own way and speak from a place of self-trust. I could see the leadership potential within them, but they would have to see it in themselves if real change was to happen.

This is a book of stories that illustrates the principles to clearer and more effective leadership communication and presence. If you've ever been told that you're too much or not enough then in these pages you will find solace. You are not too much. You are more than enough. Learn how to be more self-aware, self-confident, and present in your life and work. Become the leader that you're meant to be.

It all begins with you.

In bocca al lupo

taly, March 1993. I was hiking up a trail in the Apennine Mountain range, taking a much-needed break from my studies, the city, and the general heartbreak that's peculiar to being young. As I hiked up the trail alone, I experienced a disorientation of sorts. I could still see the small town below and the snowy trail that led me here, but I felt like I had been dropped from some distant planet. Everything felt new and strange.

I embarked on this adventure because of an uncharacteristic desire for solitude. It was the only mountain trail I knew of where I could disappear within a short hour's train ride. I left without telling my roommates where I was going, which was both unusual and unwise. I usually stayed in groups, preferring the safety of following the pack. By those standards, this hike was radical. The weather had been spring-like in the city, but when I arrived at the mountains, they were covered with a thick gob of snow. Everything around me looked like wedding cake. I was poorly dressed for hiking, with Lee jeans, secondhand wool knit sweater, thin Columbia Sportswear poncho, and cheap Timberland "walking shoes." Even so, I felt giddy when I saw the fresh snow and irrationally confident in my decision.

Part of my confidence came from the fact that I had managed to shove a sleeping bag into my day pack. I had a vague, romantic notion that I would sleep out under the stars, the snow notwithstanding. With the sleeping bag, my pack was stuffed full, but I still managed to find a little room in it for a half-bag of trail mix, a water bottle, my journal and a dog-eared copy of Kerouac's *Dharma Bums.* Just the "essentials." I had come to Italy with this notion that I could find my true, adventurous self. As I made my way up the trail, I felt that I was finally acting on that notion.

My heart lifted as my feet sank deep into the fresh snow. There were no other footprints heading up or down, which meant that I was on my own. I reached a small clearing with a ledge that overlooked the town and the surrounding mountain range. From here the trail continued up the mountain, but there was also a small path that led into some woods. I remember wishing I had brought a camera to capture the brilliant sea of white that coated the mountainside and valley. As I stood there taking it all in, I felt some kind of presence pass behind me.

When I turned around, I caught sight of the loping gait of a wolf-like animal disappear behind an Evergreen tree, only a stone's throw from where I stood. Adrenaline took over my body as my nervous system went into full fight or flight. My intestines curled and turned cold, and my mind raced. I remember turning my gaze blankly back towards the view of the town, hoping that

I could ignore the danger away. I felt like a small child closing his eyes to hide from the monsters in his room. When I was 7 years old, our family dog had attacked me, biting me several times in the face. I will never forget the sound of his growl and teeth ripping my flesh. I stood there, staring out at the distant town below, feeling the dreaded anticipation of that sound once more.

I'm not sure how long I stood, frozen on that mountainside, but eventually I got tired of waiting and gathered the courage to turn around and investigate. Emptiness. I felt relief, then irritation. Did I imagine the whole thing? I made my way over to the trees and spotted the heavy paw tracks in the snow. They had circled the tree, then headed back towards the woods. I stood there in the silence of the mountain and attempted to calm my body. What just happened?

The shadow.

Jungian psychologists talk about the power that the unconscious has on our actions and how important it is to face our "shadow self," meaning that part of ourselves that we would like to cut out or repress. Whatever part of us that we wish to repress, or reject will show up in our work and in our life in the form of relationships, obstacles, or patterns. In the book *Why We Meditate,* Tsoknyi Rinpoche refers to a similar kind of phenomenon as "beautiful monsters." These are those emotions or beliefs that we try to avoid or suppress. These might be feelings of inadequacy, unlovableness, or insecurity, which can show up in moments of vulnerability like change or growth. His advice is to meet those thoughts and feelings in meditation and to do it with compassion, to "shake hands" with the beautiful monsters.

Il lupo.

In Italy I'd learned that the Italian expression for good luck is, "In bocca al lupo," which literally translates to *into the mouth of the wolf*. Much like the theater expression "break a leg," you might say it to someone who is about to take an exam, interview for a job, or go on an adventure. It's my favorite Italian saying in part because it captures the general experience people seem to have whenever they're about to go through a major life change. It's as though they come up against some invisible obstacle that guards the threshold between who they are now and who they want to be. In my experience, this barrier is essentially some internal belief or story that they've told themselves about what's possible for them.

When I was a kid, I had an unusual awareness of when the adults around me were struggling to trust themselves, and I often could intuitively understand what was holding them back. I sensed their internal struggle and found it fascinating. As I got older, I learned that I wasn't immune to this struggle myself. I had my own insecurities, beliefs, and "beautiful monsters" following me around, and I tried just as hard as everyone else to ignore, reject, or repress them.

The older I got, the more interested I became in our capacity as people to change. What does it take to be confident in one's own skin? Can this be learned? Why do some people appear natural in front of a crowded room, while others seem nervous and fragile? Are these fixed states, or could they be changed? Can presence be taught? If so, how? Can we learn to speak with our authentic voice and with authority, regardless of the situation or the audience? Yes. The answer is yes.

When I was in college, I had been studying to be an actor. I found that I had a natural talent for the art, but there was something mysterious that kept me from feeling free on the stage. I was too self-conscious. I felt frustrated when my directors and acting teachers encouraged me to "let go" and just trust myself. I couldn't do it. Every time I stepped on stage, I felt like I was watching myself, trying to correct every mistake as they happened, and trying too hard to get it "right." I kept thinking that I would let go if I could only see what I was holding onto. It was as if there were this doorway that everyone wanted me to walk through that to them seemed so obvious, but to me felt impossible. I would get right up to the door and then look for another way around. This internal struggle continued until the last show I performed in college my senior year. I was in a one-act play where I was the main character, and normally I would have made it really complicated for myself. For whatever reason, I just stepped into the role. I let go. I stood on that stage entirely present and in my body.

It was amazing.

And I had no idea how I did it.

After graduating from college, I took a job teaching English at a private high school and enjoyed a fifteen-year career as an English and theater teacher to high school students. Teaching is an incredible way to learn about yourself, if you're willing to pay attention. I spent many years encouraging the students to be brave, trust their voices, and take chances with their writing and their acting.

They were self-conscious and afraid of something that only they could see. I noticed how they would twist their body into a pretzel shape or mumble their way through a scene, anything to avoid having to claim their full voice. I recognized all these behaviors. They were the same things that I did.

What was happening to us?

Turns out, so many things were happening. For example, I started to notice a habit I had of tucking my feet under my chair whenever I started to talk in faculty meetings. It was as if I were trying to shrink myself in the room. If you had asked me at the time, I would have told you it just felt good. What I came to realize, however, is that whenever my feet were under the chair, I lost authority in the room. There was something about this that robbed me of *presence*. When I stopped doing it, people started to listen. My voice was clearer, and I felt more confident.

Something was happening.

The physical stuff was relatively easy to change in part because it was so obvious. All it takes to show someone how they make their presence small is to take a video of them while they are speaking. Hands in pockets, arms crossed, head down, eyebrows furrowed, all show a clear depiction of the ways that we shrink ourselves. There's no way, however, to video the thoughts in our heads. The real opportunity is to change the stories in our heads.

If I had to articulate what these wolves are that prowl the doorways between who we are and who we're meant to be, it would be "stories." We all carry with us a narrative about who we are and who we should be. These myths keep us caged and trapped from moving forward. When I was a teacher working with students, I used to encourage them to trust their voices, take a chance, be wrong, discover themselves in the process, and I could watch as their stories, these wolves, would show up to shut them down. "I'm not good at public speaking." "I'm just not a good thinker." "I can't act." All these stories seem to be there to keep them in check. The worst were the ones that told them they had to be perfect. Nothing makes us more afraid to trust ourselves like the belief that we can't make a mistake.

Let me pause here and say that our stories aren't the problem in themselves. Whatever myth or belief you've had about yourself, it's probably served you well until now. Most people develop these stories because of bad experiences they had when they were young. The problem is that those stories, those myths, those habits, interfere with your ability to change and grow. If you want to learn how to claim your voice in a meeting, you will have to let go of the belief that you're not good at speaking up in public. Change is hard. Changing how you communicate yourself to others is both hard and terrifying. To be seen and heard clearly and as you are, you must be willing to let go of these things that have protected you. We have be willing to trust our own authentic voice.

When people ask me why I left teaching, I usually say that I just felt like I had to do something different. It began to feel like a sweater that I had outgrown. This is true, but I also realized that the work that I really wanted to do was around helping people find their voice and their power. I tried to do this kind of work with my young students, but I realized that it was unfair to ask seventeen-year-olds to become more aware of patterns that were just barely forming. How can they let go of a story that's still working for them? Many of them had habits that kept them safe, and much as I did when I was their age, they have reasons for wanting to protect themselves.

Adults, however, were often wonderfully fed-up with their stuckness. They had spent years trying to do it the old ways, and they recognized that they were having the same challenges in meetings or job interviews. Why were they being disregarded? Why were people telling them that they were too much?

Why were their ideas not heard, understood nor appreciated? Why were they thought of as being "too aggressive" or "too meek?" What was happening to them? What were they doing to themselves? I knew I could help them. I could see the patterns and habits that got in their way. I could hear the stories that kept them from taking a step forward and trusting themselves more fully. If they were willing to drop the behaviors that kept them safe and begin to communicate from a more authentic, clear, and meaningful place. They needed to face their wolf.

Back to that mountain in Italy.

I left the wolf tracks behind and attempted to climb the icy trail. I slipped and slid on my stomach a few dozen feet, wondering if I would ever stop. My descent was stopped abruptly by a set of trees along the edge of a small ravine. I laid there in the snow, and as if coming out of a drunken haze, I took a sober look at my situation.

My jeans were now soaking wet, and the sun that had kept me warm enough all day was moving lower in the sky. I was cold, shaking. For the first time it occurred to me that one could twist an ankle or break an arm out here. And even though I didn't know anything about hypothermia, I could feel a deep chill nagging at my body. I began to ask myself an important question. Did I really expect to sleep out here? And while I didn't want to let Kerouac down, I also thought that sleeping bag or no sleeping bag, this would be a stupid way to die.

I started walking down the mountain, ultimately breaking into a falling, sliding jog—if I hurried, I could make the last train home. Despite all that stumbling and anxiety, I also felt the thrill of some greater awareness. Once I boarded the train, I sat down by the heaters and tried to warm myself, reflecting on all that just happened. I felt as though I had stumbled onto something profound and important, but I wasn't sure what. It took years to realize that this had been an *invitation*. Whenever we take a step towards our true selves, the "wolf" will show up. The idea is to face the fear and make friends with these stories, habits, and beliefs. Take a step towards them, knowing that there's no other way to the other side of that doorway except to step into the wolf.

In the following stories, my clients are surprised to find that they might have an entrenched communication habit, and they are faced with an opportunity to choose: do they have the courage to turn and face the wolf, or do they cling to their old beliefs? I've tried to show you the vulnerability and exceptional courage they possess as they turn toward the wolf and drop their old habits. It's my wish that you'll see some of yourself in these stories and recognize their courage as your own. There's more within each of us than we sometimes dare to imagine. If you're reading this book, you've most likely already reached a high level of achievement. What's next is for you to be free from whatever is holding you back and to discover a new level of yourself in the world. May you learn from this book what it takes to speak up and be heard. May you step *into the* wolf.

Part 1 — Mateo

"What you are shouts so loudly in my ears I cannot hear what you say."

—RALPH WALDO EMERSON

CHAPTER 1

What are you protecting?

Sometimes people are so passionate, so determined to drive change, that they can create a culture of resistance and animosity. It doesn't matter how sincere your intentions are, people will experience that intensity as aggression. In this story, you will meet Mateo, a young, passionate, and talented young leader who has worked himself into a ball of frustration at his job. He has frustrated his CEO, his team, and ultimately himself so much so that it is beginning to look as though he can't do the job. What will it take for him to change? What would happen if he were willing to become more aware of his own story and how he communicates that to others? What would happen if he stopped trying to protect himself from being seen?

Mateo's burly frame fills the doorway of my Portland office. He comes in, hangs up his Carhartt raincoat, and places his boots in the corner by the door. As the youngest-ever Head of

Operations at a food processing plant in Massachusetts, he exudes a cocksureness and sense of mastery. His emotions seem to vacillate, however, between frustration and sadness, like someone who is consistently disappointed by the world around him. His demeanor is intense, and it's difficult to resist getting defensive in his presence. We've been working on softening his expressions and opening his body posture. However, given how he looks this morning, I'd say that we're not going to make much headway on that today.

Mateo's boss, Brian, the forward-thinking owner of the plant, was the one who reached out to me to do some communication coaching for Mateo. Brian hired him a year ago to improve their operations, and Mateo's impact was immediate. He improved the overall quality and efficiency of the plant in a matter of a few weeks. Brian also was eager to have Matteo tackle some of their turnover issues, which were tied to the old, "command and control" culture of the past. To be successful in changing this, Mateo needed to win over the other managers, who often chafed against new ideas. There was a battle brewing in the leadership team, and Mateo wasn't helping his cause with his rigidity and aggressive style.

Brian called me a month ago to complain, "He's brilliant, but everything he says feels like a personal attack. Even when I want to agree with him, it can feel like I'm going to war."

My impression is that Mateo is sensitive and has a lot of raw emotions under the surface. He defaults to an aggressive stance, which probably is only to protect himself. To everyone else though, it looks like anger and judgment, not a great recipe for trust.

Mateo tosses a camping knife and a ring of keys on the table and says, "They're hopeless." The clatter on the table punctuates the disgust in his voice.

"Who?" I ask, as I hand him a glass of water and take the seat across the table from him.

"The team. I gave my presentation this morning." He arranges his pen, pencil and knife neatly in line with his notebook and sips absent-mindedly at the water.

"Didn't go so well?"

Putting down the water, he crosses his arms and juts out his chin—one of those characteristics that communicates a defensive aggression. I fight the urge to also cross my arms. "Well, the general consensus is that people felt," he makes quotation marks with the fingers of his right hand, "*attacked*."

I note the petulant tone in his voice, which surprises me a little. While he's often an emotional guy, he doesn't usually take rejection personally. "What happened?"

Looking a little like a worn-out school principal, he sighs and leans his body heavily over the table. "I showed them the recent employee engagement survey and all hell broke loose. Nobody wants to hear the truth."

I know that he wants to complain about the team (and in his defense, they have their moments), but there's something else going on here. I try to guide him to the details.

"What did the survey say?"

He sits back in his chair and stretches his legs out in front of him, placing his hands behind his head. This is his "arrogant" posture, and he smiles a little as he gets ready to tell me, but the pain in his eyes tell a different story. "78% of employees say they don't trust their managers. 64% believe that their safety isn't the highest priority in the plant."

I knew he was worried about what this survey would find, but this is pretty awful. "Oh Mateo, that's such a disappointment! You must feel terrible. I'm so sorry. How did everyone else react?"

His eyes water a little as he folds his legs and arms back into himself, the arrogance melting away. These numbers hurt him more than he's willing to admit. "They didn't believe the data. Worse, they spent a lot of the time making excuses for the answers. It wasn't a productive discussion."

One thing that I admire about Mateo is that he's fearless about feedback, regardless of whether he's giving it or receiving it. Most of us secretly want only to be appreciated, not evaluated. We say we want feedback, when what we really want is a pat on the back. That's not Matteo. He is only interested in improving himself, and he gets upset when people try to flatter him with praise. In the same vein, it takes a lot for him to praise others, which wears on his managers. His brusqueness and determination for excellence can come across as judgmental and borderline cruel. On Mateo's side, he takes their resistance to his suggestions personally.

In my experience, when we feel resistance from others, especially those we work with, it's a good time to look at what's happening inside of ourselves. Often times we are pushing or trying to control others with our words. In general, we are more likely to resist other people than we are ideas. In other words, we say that we disagree with *what* people are saying, when we are most likely disagreeing with *who* is saying it.

"That sounds frustrating," I say, trying to stay neutral and grounded, even though I can feel his emotions churning. I have met the rest of the team and can imagine how defensive they might get. However, the idea that they would offer excuses surprises me. They pride themselves on a culture of "no excuses," and they all talk about their teams as though they were family. There's more to this. "I find it surprising that the team wasn't upset themselves about the employees not feeling safe."

He sits back in his chair, poking at his notebook with his pen. "Well, I may have provoked them a little."

Ah, and there it is.

Usually when someone admits being a "little" anything, they're under-reporting by a lot.

I raise my eyebrows and smile. "What exactly did you say?"

I see his jaw clench as he folds his arms across his barrel chest. "You know the saying, 'if everyone you meet today is an asshole, maybe you're the asshole?' "

I nod cautiously.

"Well, I titled the feedback slide, *Maybe you're the asshole.*" He pauses and give me an expectant smile. My hand unconsciously goes to my mouth. I'm both stopping myself from sympathetically smiling back and internally reacting to some desire to stop him from having said that. My unspoken thought is, Well, that's one way to start a fight.

"Let me ask you, Mateo," I focus on putting aside any judgment of him and focus instead on being curious, "what did you want them to feel?"

He tenses up little, perhaps surprised by the question.

"I don't know." He stares down at his hand and makes a fist. "I guess I wanted their full attention."

"Well, 'Mission accomplished'" I smile broadly, but the lightness I intended doesn't quite land.

"Right." He lets out a laugh that sounds hollow and tight. "It's hard to explain," he says while shifting in his seat, folding his arm across his stomach and bringing his fist to his chin. "They just need to get on the same page and stop being so stubborn."

There it is. *They just need to get on the same page.* There's something about this saying that brings a sense of desperation and brittleness. We so badly want to control how other people behave that we can't see how tightly we're gripping them.

I take a risk and nudge us to a more vulnerable space. "What do you notice about your body?"

"What do you mean?" He tries to sound casual, but his whole body stiffens.

I gesture with an open hand to his fist by his chin. "Are you thinking about punching someone?"

He frowns and opens up his palms, then lowers them into his lap. "Sorry. I can get intense sometimes."

I think to myself, *sometimes?* And he gives me a smile as though hearing my thoughts.

I start to think about where I want to go from here. It's important that self-awareness feels like an invitation, not a judgment. I don't want him to turn all this intensity into self-judgment. It's also true that you can't convince anyone to let down his or her guard. Sometimes though, if I let down *my* defenses a little, there's a chance (just a chance) the other might. It doesn't take much for me to see what I'm defending against. I'm afraid of upsetting him. I'm trying to dance around the conversation, hoping that he will invite me in, but he's well-defended. Better to just be direct.

"Would you like," I ask, "to know how I experience you in these moments?"

He gives his shoulders a shrug, "Sure."

Sure is one of my favorite passive-aggressive signalers. Whenever I hear *sure* instead of *yes*, it implies a kind of ambivalence. *What* exactly that ambivalence is about is not always clear. Given his usual appetite for feedback, I imagine that this ambivalence is more just not being certain where I'm going with this. Let's see what comes up.

"When you were talking about the team, I sensed that you were thinking "*I had this feeling like I was the problem.*" Does that make sense?"

He leans forward and puts his elbows on the table.

"I definitely feel that way with the team, but why did you feel that?"

"I'm not exactly sure, but it felt like you were disappointed in all of us humans. In short, it felt judgmental." I choose this word carefully to see how he reacts.

He doesn't flinch. "It's just that I'm passionate about my work. It's not personal."

I point to his clenched fists on the table in front of me. "See that?"

He shakes his hands, sits back in his chair and chuckles, "I don't even know that I'm doing it."

"Well, that's actually the problem. You're making everyone feel like they're in a fight with you. Kind of like the presentation this morning?" Mateo nods absently, and I can feel him start to go up in his head. Once you start analyzing yourself, it's really hard to get back to the present.

I swing us quickly to a solution. "What did you want them to hear this morning?"

He pulls tightly on his ponytail, almost as a physical way to bring himself back into the room. After a moment he answers with a lightness in his tone, "That we're better than this."

Perfect.

"Then all you need to do is to stop making them feel like they're enemy."

"How do I do that?"

"Well, let's start by understanding what's true."

What is true?

I t took me a long time to recognize that when people mixed personal beliefs with facts, they often created an internal confusion. It often happened when people talked about art or politics and presented their personal perspectives and beliefs as though they were objective facts. This only works if your audience already agrees with you. In most cases, no two people will look at a situation and have the exact same truth. There's almost always a gap between you and the other person, and you can't close that gap if you assume that you both see the same thing. I write two words for Mateo on the whiteboard in the room: "Truth" with a capital T, which is an objective fact, and "truth" with a lower-case t, which is more of a personal truth, an opinion. Then I turn and ask him, "What was the title of that slide again?"

Mateo clears his throat and crosses his hands across his chest. "It was, *Maybe you're the asshole?* It's a principle that I use a lot in my life. If I feel like everyone is being a jerk, then maybe I'm the jerk. I wanted to be provocative."

"Well, you definitely provoked them."

He smiles and rubs the back of his neck, which I'm guessing is a reaction to his frustration with this whole situation.

I continue, "This principle of 'Maybe you're the asshole,'" I say, "do you feel that it's a capital T truth?"

"Yes." A stubbornness comes across his face when he says this. He's not going to surrender easily. I decide not to draw attention to the fact that his behavior in this moment might be making the case for his principle.

"Principles are the truths that help us to manage ourselves better in the world, but they are difficult to prove as objective facts." I look towards the window and gesture to the storm outside. "It's raining. It doesn't matter if people *believe* it to be true or not, it's objectively true. It's delusional to believe otherwise."

He sneaks a look out the window and smiles uncertainly, "I see…"

"A lowercase truth is subjective. For example, the idea that rainy days are bad is a lowercase truth."

He smiles crookedly and tilts his head slightly, "Aren't they though?"

"That's a matter of opinion. If you're a farmer, rainy days might be a lifesaver, right?" He shrugs and his eyes glaze over a bit.

I need to bring this back to him and his team. "Okay, it's a fact that the employee survey shows that there's a 78% lack of trust in the organization's leadership, right?"

His face flushes red, "Yes, that's what it said."

"And you want them to hear that this is a reflection on the managers, right?"

"That's a capital T Truth. They need to accept it."

And that's what I'm looking for. "That's the thing, Mateo. They don't actually need to accept it. That's *your perspective.*"

He gives me a scowl of doubt and shakes his head. "Nope, that's just the truth."

"It's your truth, based on your experience and your understanding of how people think and work." I pause to take a step back and then say, "I even agree with you. Whatever is going on is most likely the result of how the managers are behaving or at least how they're being perceived."

He rubs his forehead. "If you agree with me, then what are we talking about?"

I know that he's angry now, but I think that we might be close. "It's about whether it's helpful to talk about this as an absolute Truth." I go back to the board and draw a frame. "You see, we can't really argue about the rain because it's a fact of reality. *What the rain means to us is an interpretation based on context and our frame of reference.*" I emphasize this point by writing *farmer* on the frame and the words *rain=good* inside it.

He's leaning forward in his chair, and his elbows are on his knees. His face is more relaxed. I can tell he's more focused.

The idea is clicking for him, so I keep going. "The better we are at sharing our frame (or lens through which we see an event) and speaking from our perspective, or our truth, the easier it is for others to understand what we mean. It's a way to close the gap."

He sits back and folds his arms for a quick moment, then unfolds them and brings his hands to his face. Talking through his fingers (something we often do when we are unsure of our words), he asks, "How do I get them to see that their behaviors impact the engagement score?"

This is the question that I've been waiting for. We can't close the gap in communication if we don't understand what we're trying to solve for in the first place. When you can articulate clearly what you want and why, then you have a chance at impact. His question is helpful because it's *positive*, meaning it moves the conversation forward.

"That's a good start. What if you invited them into that problem, rather than make them the problem? The more vulnerable you make yourself, the greater the chance that they will follow you."

At the word "vulnerable" he takes a step back and crosses his arms again. I decide to try a different tack. "Why does it matter to you so much that they change their behavior?"

He leans his back against the wall and looks at me. These are crucial moments in the relationship. Will he trust me enough to open up, or will he defend?

He finally steps forward and with hands in his pockets, starts talking. "When I was in high school, I worked summers and weekends at a local food processing plant in Milwaukee where my dad worked full time. My parents were immigrants, but my father was able to get a good job there and provide a good life for us. The job paid well enough, but the conditions were not great. Most of the problems came down to some bad managers. They made a hard job harder." He rests himself against the table as he's talking, and I watch as his presence noticeably shifts in the room. His voice becomes softer, and his face is more open, even though he's hugging himself as he talks.

"I was the kind of kid who liked to get into fights in my neighborhood, but I also read a lot and liked to argue. I would have been fired from the job on my first day, but the owner liked me a lot. He saw me reading a book once on a break, and we got to talking about philosophy and history. Turns out, he had wanted to study history, but he had to take over the business for his father. We traded books and he would always come down to the floor when I was working and chat." Mateo hugs himself a little tighter and looks down at the floor.

"He was the first adult, other than my parents, who talked about me going to college as a given. He encouraged me to apply, and when the financial aid wasn't enough, he gave me a scholarship from the plant so I could go." Shaking his head, he says, "I felt like a fish out of water at college, but I graduated. I guess I've always wanted to pay that forward in some way. I know that he made a difference in my life because he really saw me. I guess I feel a responsibility to bring that back to the world of operations."

He walks up to the board and points at the frame drawn there. I want managers to recognize the impact on people when they see them, *truly* see them. My dad and the other workers were treated like they didn't matter. I, for whatever reason, was seen by this one guy, and it changed my life. It's the easiest way to make a difference in a person's life."

I wait to see if there's more, but he sits back into his chair by the table.

I make my way back to the seat across from him and ask, "What if you just told them that? What if you shared your story with the rest of the team?"

He looks up at me as if to see if I'm kidding, then shakes his head. "No way. Never going to happen."

"Think about it. What do they need to change if they're going to be better managers?"

"They're going to have to be better communicators. The employees don't trust them because they don't listen."

"Great, then this story would help them see that, right?"

"I guess so, but it's really about trust. They have to trust the people who work for them." He folds his arms in a defensive posture and sits back in his chair.

That word "*trust*," it's the key ingredient to all relationships, isn't it? This time, however, I know that he's actually talking about himself.

"Do you trust *them*?"

"What do you mean?" He shifts uneasily in his chair and throws one leg over the other. His body looks like a pretzel.

"You want them to be willing to change and to trust their employees more, right?"

"Right."

"Okay, then why not trust them with your story. Let them know why this is so important to you. Shaming them won't work. Open your heart and let them in."

"Share my story. You think that will work?"

I nod. "I'd put money on it, as long as it comes from a place of self-trust, honesty and openness. I've learned not to underestimate the power of vulnerability."

CHAPTER 3

What if you surrendered?

Self-trust is hard to talk about, in part because it's often deeply correlated with overly romantic and sentimental images. I grew up thinking that "digging deep" and trusting myself had to look like that scene in *Rocky III* where Sylvester Stallone and Carl Whethers are running along the beach with "Eye of the Tiger" playing in the background. (Looking back at that scene, I guess you'd have to trust yourself a lot to wear a three-quarter t-shirt and those shorts.) Reality is much less dramatic than this, in my experience. That moment of self-trust is usually made up of a seemingly mundane decision. Do I call him back? Do I tell the truth about how I'm feeling? Do I say yes, rather than say no? It's a question of whether we open ourselves up to the world or close the world out.

Why wouldn't Mateo just share his perspective with the rest of the team? I think, at the heart of it, it had to do with fear. Fear of being rejected or of losing control. It's often a fear borne out of our experiences as kids (Seventh grade, anyone?) But it's a fear that we must be willing to push through if we're going to change. Invariably, I work with people who want the group to earn their trust before they will be vulnerable with them. While that is a reasonable desire, it can create a standoff that interferes with our own communication. If we're willing to be vulnerable (without being needy), then we have the chance to bridge those gaps.

On the Tuesday after Mateo and I last met, I texted him to see how his next leadership meeting went. We scheduled a call to debrief. Brian had asked him to apologize to the team. He needed a way to reset the conversation. I agreed with that strategy (although I worried that it might put Mateo on the defensive even more). I offered to facilitate, but Mateo insisted that he wanted to do it himself. While he knew it would be awkward, he wanted to do this without the impression of needing a safety net.

The thing with being vulnerable in a group is that you must be willing to surrender your ego. In many cases it's this fantasy of what we think "safety" is. I don't mean safe physically, but rather the idea that we keep others from seeing parts of ourselves that we don't necessarily like, or things that they may not like about us. I've seen people attempt to be vulnerable while still holding onto this idea that they can control what other's think. The result is usually that they come across sounding arrogant, defensive, or even aggressive. Mateo's a fighter, so I wasn't sure that surrendering was going to be his thing.

Now his name flashes across my phone, and I pick it up, eager to hear how it went.

"Mateo! So great to hear from you. How are you?"

His dog is recovering well from some recent surgery, and he's moving forward with buying a house, which seems like a further indication that he's getting comfortable in the job. He sounds lighter and happier on the phone than I've heard him in weeks. After a few minutes, he finally asks, "Do you want to hear how it went?"

"Um, Yes!?" There's a playfulness and lightness in his voice, which is in contrast to his usual somber attitude. I want to say something about it, but I hold my tongue. Not all observations are helpful, and this is one of those times to let him be.

"Well, it didn't start off so great." I feel him smile while he's talking, so I imagine that he's enjoying this set-up. "I think I may have started off more defended than I meant to."

I start to ask what he means by that, but quickly silence myself again. This is his story, and I need to let him tell it the way he wants to.

"So, I basically started off by saying that I have a different perspective than they do, and that I want to share it."

Okay, it's a little defensive, but I let that go.

"I told them that I'm a child of immigrants and grew up a lot like the people who work here. Then I told them that the problem was that, unlike me, they probably all grew up with some privilege and that's what was causing the misunderstanding."

My heart sinks a little. This is not a great way to start an open conversation.

"How did they react to that?" I ask, even though I have a pretty decent picture of it in my head.

"Not well. People got really upset. There was some yelling and Dan was the maddest I've ever seen. He even got up to leave."

Dan was a senior manager and usually one of Mateo's biggest supporters. Perhaps in part because he's also a bit of a hothead.

"What did you do?"

"Honestly, I wasn't sure what I'd said that was offensive. I thought I was stating the obvious."

He pauses so as not to shout over an ambulance siren that rushes past him on the street. I picture him outside his plant walking through town on a sunny spring day. After the siren dies down, he says, "Then I realized that they were feeling attacked again. I had attacked them somehow."

"How so?" I'm trying to let him lead, which is hard because I want to jump in and say so many things about how people instinctively react to judgment and assumption as though they were under attack. And how, if you want people to hear the truth, they have to believe that it comes from a place of non-judgmental caring. But I keep my mouth shut and wait for him to answer.

"I wasn't sure. At first, I wanted to prove that I was right." He stops to think about this before continuing. "I wanted to be understood, but I didn't want to be judged. So, you know, I judged them."

Wow. "And that's why they felt attacked?"

"Yes. I hadn't shared my story. Instead, I had just told them how they were wrong."

"That's right. It depends on what you wanted to happen. If you want to fight, then telling people they're wrong works well. If you want to build connections and trust, then you have to use more open and vulnerable language."

"Yeah, so we took a break to cool down, and when we came back, I told them that I was going to share my whole story, if they were willing to listen. I talked about my dad and the owner of the plant." He laughs and says, "I, uh, may even have gotten a little emotional."

Again, wow. "How did that go?"

"Awesome." And again, something in his voice tells me that he's smiling. "It was an entirely different conversation. Actually, it *was* a conversation. For the first time, we really listened to each other."

There's so much happening here that I almost feel dizzy. I don't want to mistake his analysis of this moment as fundamental change, but it's an amazing beginning. The weird thing about coaching people in this work is that I often feel the paradoxes. I know that being more vulnerable and aware works, but it's often counter-intuitive to what we *think* we need to do. It's easy to give advice, but it takes courage to do it. Mateo's willingness to be vulnerable and dig into the work is a reminder of how the work isn't just about tools or skills; it's about reminding ourselves that we want to connect, and we want to collaborate.

We are so easily wounded and hurt by each other, but if we can learn to stay present like Mateo did and reflect on our own motives, we have a chance to change the relationship. And when we're willing to let down our defenses with each other, we not only make better connections, but we also become better collaborators. It's unusual to have someone pivot so quickly like Mateo, but I suspect that he never really enjoyed the role of the fighter.

Sometimes we fight because we can't imagine any other way of being. We shut people out because it seems like the only option.

Taming the wolf:

Are your emotions secretly driving your communication? One of the most important skills to learn in communication is the ability to manage your emotions. We often think of this as pertaining only to people who are both sensitive and have a quick temper (like Mateo), but it's also important for those who tend to disconnect from their emotions. Either way, you run the risk of letting your emotions run the meeting without your permission.

If you suppress your feelings, they will leak out. The more awareness you have about what you're experiencing and the better you are at communicating that clearly without making others responsible, the more space you make for others to connect with you.

There are so many ways that we defend ourselves. One acting teacher pointed out to me that I use my smile to manage others, and this awareness helped me to radically change dynamics that I had with people in my life. We use all kinds of habits to defend ourselves: sarcasm, logic, positional authority, victimhood, self-righteousness, anger, etc… These habits tend to lead to dysfunctional teams.

Defensiveness is a way to invite resistance, and Matteo had to learn to let down his guard if he wanted his team to listen to him. In the end, all he cared about was making the plant a better place for workers. That could only be communicated from a place of trust, earned when he was willing to become honest, open, and clear.

Part 2 — Barbara

"When I walk on stage, man, all I can give them is me."

—JANIS IAN

CHAPTER 1

Why won't they let you lead?

There are many reasons why some people experience roadblocks to their promotion. I've rarely met a woman in an organization who wants her leadership to be solely identified with her gender, and yet that's what often happens. Gender bias, racism, and classism are most organizations' blind spots. For all of us in positions of power, it's important that we get curious and open-minded about how a biased framework might be impacting us in ways we don't even realize. Watch as my client, Barbara, steps out of the story of her own disempowerment and instead claims her own power and finds a way to navigate a challenging situation.

It's 6:57 am and I'm rushing up the stairs to my office for a 7 am meeting. I'm not exactly late by my standards, but Barbara is the type of client for whom "on time" is ten minutes before the appointment. She hired me to help her work on her "executive presence" and her "executive voice" as she took on more responsibilities at her bank, and we've been working together for about a year now. As I reach the top steps, she's patiently sitting on a chair outside my door, reviewing what seem to be work documents.

I offer a lighthearted, breathless apology as I unlock the door to my office, but I can see that she's distracted by something else going on.

"Nonsense, you're right on time." She doesn't look up from the folder, so I busy myself with getting the room ready and let her settle in. She's got short-cropped, silver-and-black hair and wears a variation of a dark-blue pantsuit each time we meet. Barbara was briefly an art major in college before switching to finance to satisfy her parents, and one vestige of the art major in her might be her whimsical reading glasses, which flash from a bright red chain around her neck. When I first met her, I was struck by her self-confidence. She's an expert at most things she sets her mind to and seems equally at home talking about tax law or motorcycles.

The main challenge at the beginning of our work together was that her peers at the bank were intimidated by her. They dreaded hearing her say in a meeting, "Mind if I ask a clarifying question?" because they knew her questions sometimes/often left the presenter's assumptions (and sometimes their dignity) in shreds. There was a sharpness to her tone that made it hard for others to hear her. Barbara's self-defense was that she grew a thick skin doing art critiques in school and was often amazed now at how sensitive other people could be.

Yet in the past year she's softened her communication style and improved her relationship with her peers so much that she's been seriously considered as the successor to the CEO. I hadn't seen her since she emailed me that she was up for the position, so I take the time this morning to congratulate her in person.

She says thank you, but her smile is tight.

"Barbara, is something going on?"

She rolls her eyes in the chair across from me and places her mug on the floor. "Oh, nothing much. Just that the board decided at the last minute to only approve the position of 'interim' CEO." She smiles. "They expressed their 'full' support but had some 'concerns' about how I'll 'manage' in this new role." With each quote from the board, she makes jabbing quotation marks in the air with her fingers. Despite her sarcasm (or maybe because of it), the hurt feelings are obvious.

I'm upset for her as well, but I suppose I shouldn't be too surprised. This transition process has been eerily smooth up to this point, and we'd talked about ways that things could go sideways. But neither of us figured on the Board taking a different turn at the last minute.

"What happened?"

"Okay," she lifts the chain of her reading glasses and curls it around her finger. "So last night's meeting was supposed to be the official vote on my becoming CEO. It was really a formality. I already was doing the job, but the Chair wanted to take this moment to...." She pauses to search the ceiling for the right phrase, "'recalibrate expectations.'"

"What does that mean?"

"Who knows? He complimented me on my leadership through the past several months while Dale was out." Dale has been the CEO for the past 15 years, and he was planning on retiring soon.

"The Chair even mentioned how much better the bank's performance has been since I've been running operations."

"So, what were his concerns?"

"It gets better. He said, 'I'm so glad that we could be an *advocate* for you. We're so proud of how much you've *grown* here at this bank.' Grown!" she says again, "as if I were a child prodigy and not the woman who has steered them through this mess."

She and I already had talked a whole lot about the misogyny she'd experienced in the banking world throughout her career, and Barbara had been hoping that this smaller bank would be different. Dale, the prior CEO, had brought her into the company with the intention that she'd be his replacement. He had empowered her to take on important strategic initiatives, and the Board had been happy to go along with Dale's lead, until now.

I decide to ask the obvious question. "Do you still want the job?"

"I don't know." She sighs and offers a shrug. "Why won't they just let me lead?"

Good question.

"Do you mean aside from sexism?" I ask.

She laughs and shakes her head. "I've experienced that my whole career. This feels different. It feels personal."

How could it not? Thinking that it's personal, however, is a guaranteed way to feel stuck.

As if she could hear my thoughts, Barbara says, "I just want some clarity on how to move forward with this."

"What if we broke it into three components?" I jump up to the whiteboard and draw three columns. I label the first one "Facts," the second "Emotions," and the third "Story." Then I turn to her and ask, "What are the facts of what happened?"

"They decided to wait to officially make me CEO."

I write "Held back" in the Facts column. "Okay, and what emotion did you feel when they did this?"

"Honestly? I've never been so pissed in my life."

I smile and write "angry!" in the Emotions column and then hesitate before asking, "do you think that you might also have felt hurt?" I know that this is a more provocative word, and wait to see if she deflects, but she doesn't shy away from it.

"Definitely," she says as she walks up to the board with me.

I write "hurt" next to "angry" and move over to the Story column.

"And what story are you telling yourself?"

Her eyes scan the columns, her face a closed-door to her emotions. After a moment she says, "That they don't believe I can do it."

CHAPTER 2

Are you aware of the story you're in?

There are two things happening here with Barbara. First, the board is making a huge mistake in treating her like a teenager who's asking for the keys to their Corvette. I recognize that they think they're doing the responsible thing, but it feels like a miss, (a paternalistic and sexist one) especially after she's already proven herself capable. but it's unlikely that the Board is aware of that. It's their very lack of awareness that creates a big risk that they will lose her. Second, and most important to our work, Barbara feels like *she* isn't trusted to lead, creating a story of self-doubt in her which could undermine her ability to be a great leader.

Since I don't get to work with the Board (and they aren't looking for my opinion), I will have to focus on Barbara. She has agency here; we just need figure out where it is.

"Barbara, how old did you feel when the Chair said he wanted to make you interim?"

This isn't the first time that I've asked her to name how old she felt in a situation, so she knows what to look for. It was only a few years ago that I began to notice for myself how certain situations could make me *feel* like a child in my own life, and the way that feeling affected my thoughts and communication.

"Oh God," Barbara says now, "it was like I was fourteen again and the only girl in Mr. Dubois' honors geometry class. I left that class every day feeling stupid."

Okay, now the goal is to change the story she is telling herself.

"But you stuck it out, right?"

She tucks her feet under her chair, which makes her seem a little smaller.

"Barely. I was so glad there were no geometry requirements in my Finance major." She's shrinking and I'm not sure what's going on. This is clearly a big memory.

Maybe if we can be more detached from these emotions, we can see a way through it. "What are you feeling right now?"

It's often hard to name emotions, but again Barbara doesn't flinch.

"I feel awful. I don't know, is small a feeling?"

While "small" might not be an emotion, it does hint at shame. Shame is a big word, but it is often at the heart of stories like the one with Mr. Dubois. It's the archetypal story that tells you that *you don't belong* or *you're not enough.*

I nod. "I think I understand what you mean in this case." I point to her feet and ask, "Do you notice what you're doing there?"

She shoots her feet out straight from under her chair and looks slightly embarrassed. "What was I doing?"

"Well, you were actually making yourself small." I tuck my own feet under my chair to show her. "When we contract our body, especially when we're feeling small already, we send a signal to ourselves and to others that we are, in fact, small."

She looks up from her feet and gives me a frustrated look. "Why do I do that?"

"Well, I think that it has something to do with how safe you feel. When your teacher said that about girls and geometry, he brought a sexist narrative to the classroom. He made you a someone who didn't belong."

A shake of her head as she stops herself from tucking her feet back under the chair. "But I did belong."

"Right. But I think it's difficult to try to hold our personal story at the same time someone in authority is imposing a different one on us, especially when we're kids. So, we do our best to shrink our presence so that we can stay safe. It's like a way to be there and not be there."

When people become aware of the story they're living, sometimes it can bring about a kind of paralysis. So I wait to see how she reacts. Barbara seems to be settling into this concept. Eventually she starts nodding her head. "I feel like I have to hold these two confusing truths in my head at the same time--I belong, and they don't think I belong."

"Do you feel like that teacher from high school didn't want you to succeed?"

"Sort of. I felt like he thought I was making a mistake."

"If you could go back in time and talk to yourself, what would you say?"

She smiles as she playfully waves her foot in the air. "I'd tell her to forget about him. She's going to kick-ass in college." There's a gleeful, rebellious look that flashes across her face.

"What if you could tell yourself not to worry about what this Board thinks today? What if you just skipped right to the ass-kicking?"

I'm deadpan when I say this, but she laughs and sits up in her chair. "That last part. That's what I want."

"Then let's talk about how you can communicate from that place and ignore all the other distractions."

CHAPTER 3

What if you accepted yourself?

When we stop looking for validation outside ourselves, we open up to the power of our own presence. That's what I see possible for Barbara, once she's able to let go of what the Board is signaling. One of the gifts of a good leader is that she believes she belongs on the big stage, no matter what the audience might say or do. She is able to ignore the self-doubt when it comes up, because she knows it doesn't serve the moment.

Barbara and I take a short break to stretch and move around. Now she seems her usual, confident self. As soon as she sits back down in her chair, however, some thought darkens her mood, and she begins to shrink again. I decide to start here.

"Barbara, what are you thinking about now?"

She gives a tight smile. "I was trying to figure how I could convince them to trust me."

"Do you trust yourself?"

There's a flash of something in her smile, anger? She shakes her head no but says, "Of course."

I fight an impulse to point out that her body disagrees with her words. "This is a moment you have been wanting for a long time, yes?"

"Definitely." She nods slowly, but there's tension in her voice as she says it.

"And if you were to guess, what were your expectations going into the Board meeting last night?"

She shrugs and I notice two physical reactions: her arms are folded across her chest, and she's shrunk a little in her chair again. Something is up, and I want to tread lightly.

"If it had been me," I say, "I would've gone in expecting that I already had the title."

"Well, I should have known that nothing in life is certain. It is their prerogative."

"True, but it's still disappointing."

"I should have known that they weren't going to just hand it over."

There's that word again, *should*. I can feel her folding into herself. Whenever we start "should-ing" ourselves, our presence and confidence start to disappear. Her eyes lose focus and drift.

I ask her, "Is there anyone else at the bank more ready than you to step into this role?"

Her attention comes back to me, and she thinks about this question seriously before saying, "No, Dale was clear that he needed someone from outside the bank."

"Excellent. And he picked you to be that person, right?"

A smile begins to form on her lips as she slowly nods her head. "Well, yes, but obviously the Board has doubts."

"Yes, obviously." I leave a little pause for dramatic effect. "I suppose the real question is whether *you* have the same doubts?"

She sighs in frustration and throws her head back in her chair. "I just want them to let me do my job. We're going to make this the best bank in the region. Why won't they let me?"

Why won't they let me?

That's the key question, right? Why won't they trust me? Why don't they believe me? Why are they blocking me? All of those questions are familiar to anyone who has had to fight to be heard. Again, how does Barbara get agency here? How can she claim her voice? First, we need to deal with the doubt.

CHAPTER 4

What is self-trust?

"Let's take a moment to put aside why the Board won't let you lead the way you want and instead try to answer the question I asked. Why do you think that you doubt yourself?" There are times when I ask a question that I sense might be crossing a line, but I know it's the right question to ask and a risk worth taking, if I think it might move us forward and as long as I'm not being judgmental.

Barbara's face becomes serious, and all the lightness and warmth go out of her voice. "I don't doubt myself."

Uh oh. I better be careful here. I lean a little in my chair, feeling the tension, and she subtly mimics this movement.

I say, "I can only speak for myself here, but I sometimes look to others to trust me so that I can trust myself more. The question we could ask here is whether you *need* their permission to be a leader."

"I need *them* to support me, or I *won't* be successful." Her tone is sharp on the words "them" and "won't."

I lean away from her a little to let out the tension. There's a difference here that I'm trying to articulate. "What if you acted *as if* they already supported you? What if you saw their indecision, not as a commentary on your ability, but rather as a statement on their own insecurity? How might that change your attitude?"

She looks out the window at the clouds going by and then back at me. "I guess I would just get back to work." She pauses to write something down on her notebook, and then says matter-of-factly, "You know, it occurs to me that they didn't fight me on any of the goals I put forth in my plan."

"Interesting. Why is that?"

"I don't know. They're ambitious goals. I was so distracted though, by the 'interim' title, that I didn't even think about how they were just letting me do what I want."

"Yeah, this doesn't excuse the fact that they blindsided you with their own fear and most likely their own sexism. But what if you didn't feel as though you had to solve for that?"

She sighs and lets out the tension that's been in the room for the past ten minutes. "That's it? Trust myself and everything will work out?"

"Well," I hesitate a little, "you make it sound easy. In my experience it isn't easy at all. If we want to trust ourselves more as leaders, if we really want to step through that door, we have to recognize some of the illusions we cling to."

"And what's that for me?"

I shrug. "You know better than I do, but I can tell you what's on the other side."

She offers a huge smile, settles deeper into her chair and asks, "What's that?"

"The simple truth that you're the right person for this job." Something important feels unsaid. Then it occurs to me: "And that nobody belongs here more than you."

She thinks for a moment before asking, "So what do I tell them?"

"Right. Let's figure out what you want from them moving forward. If you really are going to meet the goals you laid out, it's only right that they offer you a path to the role. Let's be direct in asking for that."

She writes something else down in her notebook before asking, "What if they don't listen?"

Isn't it true that when we have to depend on other people, our biggest fear is often that they won't listen to us? "Let's clear all the ways they might not hear you from your communication, and then see what happens. My guess is that they just have some growing-up to do, and you're going to help them."

Taming the wolf:

There are two kinds of stories going on in any given moment. First there's the story you're telling yourself, and then there's the story the other party is projecting onto you. The better you are at understanding your own story and what role you are playing in it (the three most iconic and well-traveled roles are victim, villain, hero), the easier it is to notice how you might be caught up in their projection. If you can clear your own illusions, then you WILL be able to see through theirs.

Barbara heard the story that she wasn't "enough," and it dovetailed with her own self-doubt. Detaching from both stories allowed her the chance to look more closely at the facts of the situation: *the bank needed her more than she needed them.* Our job is to make sure that we don't muddy the water by inadvertently bringing our own inner story of insecurity, fear and self-doubt into it. Clear the water and then you can deal with what's there.

There's a lot that a group can do to make people feel that they don't belong. We are social animals, and the fear of rejection is real. Belonging is also something that we can radiate from within. When we purposely or inadvertently ask permission to belong, it takes all the power away from us. Groups (like Boards) are often made up of human beings who are just as insecure and wounded as everyone else, and they tend to react aversely to insecurity or neediness.

Acting "as if" you already belong by silencing the self-doubt and quieting the body can help you convey a sense of confidence. This is true, even if you still hear those inner doubts in your head. They are just thoughts. If you ever find yourself wondering if you belong, the answer is yes, always yes.

Part 3 — Sandeep

"To be what I am. To live the life that was set for me to live. To voice the things only I can voice. To bear the blossoms that are commanded of my heart. This is what I want and surely this cannot be presumptuous."

—RANIER MARIA RILKE

CHAPTER 1

How are you perceived?

There are times when, like Barbara, we encounter resistance because of bias. There are also times when it's because we haven't earned the full trust of our peers. For technical people like Sandeep, it is the latter. It can be difficult to communicate all that you know and understand in a way that others can hear you. This is especially true if your position, like IT, is at a crossroads in the organization. You have to take big strategic ideas and make them a reality, which creates friction in the organization when people have to deal with the limitations of their ideas. How do you work with the resistance you experience and not take it personally?

As I enter the cafeteria of his large insurance company in Boston, I see Sandeep sitting in the back corner talking to Vinay, one of his direct reports. Sandeep is the newly appointed "Interim" CIO, and I've been working with him for the past year in preparation for this transition to full CIO. The title "interim" was not what he wanted, but he's hoping that with a little more coaching he can win over the Executive team and Board.

He waves me over to his booth. I recognize Vinay from a workshop we did a year ago. He is a technically brilliant young man in charge of their SAP system, whom Sandeep has been mentoring. Vinay smiles and waves at me before shyly packing up his things. Sandeep says something to him, and he laughs and heads out.

Sandeep gestures for me to sit and says with a broad smile, "I told him that he's next for coaching. If I can do it, he can." He rolls a plastic bottle of water between the palms of his hands and gives me an expectant look. "What do you have planned for me today?"

I smile at his teasing since he knows that I don't plan our talks. I like to trust that whatever is going on with the client is probably exactly what we need to work on. I decide to start with a question: "How did your last enterprise strategy session go? Did people like your suggestion?"

Sandeep is a fantastic leader of teams. His relationship with Vinay is just one of many examples of his ability to connect with the people who work for him. He is both warm and thoughtful in his communication as well as rigorous and persistent. He does, however, need people to think that he's smart and good at his job, and this leads to over explanation and complex language when dealing with his peers. They often act like they don't trust him (or maybe they just feel threatened). Either way, it's a problem.

"It went well, yes." His voice sounds confident, but his eyes stay focused on the table. "Larry loved my idea for creating a new Digital Architecture Program across the company." Larry is the

CEO who chose to promote Sandeep, against the wishes of the other Senior Executives.

"Well, we knew that Larry would like it, but how did the others take it?"

Sandeep's dark eyes narrow as he shakes his head. "I don't think they understood the idea. One person on the team even accused IT of making a power grab." He doesn't say who the person is, but I have a pretty good sense that it was the Chief Marketing Officer, Tom, who has come up in quite a few of our conversations.

In Sandeep's eyes, Tom is either blocking an IT idea or he's putting forth strategies that undermine current programs. It doesn't help that Tom is more seasoned in internal politics than Sandeep.

"What did Larry say?" I ask this knowing that even though Larry likes this idea, he has already initiated a lot of change and might not push this too hard.

"Nothing," and then his voice trails off. "He wants us to talk it through…"

All the energy leaves Sandeep's body, and his presence visibly shrinks. He looks defeated. What is it about Tom that pushes his buttons so much?

"Sandeep, what's the biggest criticism of your Digital Architecture idea?"

He looks at me and shrugs his shoulders. "I'm not really sure."

A group of people meeting a few tables over laughs loudly, and he looks over at them before saying, "It feels personal."

That's the problem, isn't it? Even when we know it's just business, it can feel so personal. When it feels that way, it's hard to know where the criticism of your idea ends and the criticism of you begins. My intuition is to ignore the personal comment (too heady to try to explain) and instead dive into the details.

"Was there one thing that Tom and the others said that they didn't like?"

"That's it. They didn't talk about the idea at all. They kept talking about what happened with the Salesforce integration last year. I tried to explain that this was supposed to fix those problems from now on, but they wouldn't listen."

They wouldn't listen.

That's probably the most common complaint that I hear from clients. This epidemic called not listening is usually the result of two people arguing on different tracks and staying resolutely unwilling (or often unable) to switch tracks and meet the other person where they are. Sandeep wants to talk about the future, and Tom wants to talk about the past. No wonder they couldn't hear each other.

"Let's try something Sandeep." I lean into the table a little to close the gap between us. "What did you *want* them to hear?"

I use this question as a way to get people to uncover what they really want to say. Years ago, I watched a mentor use this phrase with a room full of scientists who were struggling to gain clarity in their incredibly technical and complicated message. This simple question cleared away the fog and helped them move forward. Let's see if it works with Sandeep.

He leans his elbows on the table and puts his fingers together into a tent shape. "What I wanted them to understand was..."

I interrupt: "not *understand,* but what you wanted them to *hear.* There's a difference."

There's the slightest frustration in his eyes. In a flat tone he says, "Exactly what I said-- *that we want to create an architecture committee that reviews and plans out how we will integrate technology into the enterprise system in a way that best ensures a positive outcome for the business uses.*"

"That's what you *said*, but I'm guessing that isn't what Tom or the others heard." I can see that he's not buying it, and I recognize from experience this can be a confusing concept for someone who is as rational as Sandeep. Why would anyone interpret his words differently than how he meant them?

I try to clarify. "I'm going to guess that what Tom heard in that statement is different than you intended."

"How so?"

"Given his history with IT, I'm guessing that what he heard was something along the lines of 'You want to take control of all my business decisions as it relates to technology.'"

A look of horror crosses his face, and he exclaims, "That's not what I meant at all!"

"Okay then, what did you want him to hear?" I mentally cross my fingers, hoping that repeating the question won't frustrate him more.

He rubs his face and thinks about the question again before saying, "that we want to help with their success, and not be an obstacle to it."

"And this committee would be a way to help you do that?"

"Absolutely. The reason that the Salesforce integration didn't go well is that IT was brought in at the project very late. We could have saved them a lot of trouble had we been involved earlier in the conversation. They need to trust us."

His voice goes up an octave, revealing his anxiety and frustration. There's some history here as well, which contributes to the lack of trust. My main objective is not to solve what's happened, it's to give Sandeep something proactive to do.

"It sounds like you need to share your lens."

CHAPTER 2

What is your lens?

Sandeep opens his glasses case and pulls out a set of reading glasses.

"How long have you been using those?" I ask him. I can't resist the chance to use such a perfect metaphor when it's right in front of me.

"About a month. I'm not used to them yet." He holds them up and looks at me through the lenses.

"Sandeep when I use the word 'lens' I'm really talking about your individual view on the world. Nobody will ever know what the world looks like through your eyes and vice versa."

He nods but then looks down like he's trying to read something on his shoes. I sense he's not getting it. I try again.

"We each have these thoughts, biases, experiences and perceptions that we have about the world. They change how we look at situations and how we interpret opportunities. No matter how hard we try though, we can't get away from this lens. The best that we can do is to improve how we talk about what we see so that others can have the chance to see the same."

He unfolds his arms, and his shoulders come down a bit while he returns his glasses back to their case. "I'm guessing I'm bad at sharing my lens, then, huh?"

"Not *bad*, just unused to it. Until now, your job didn't really depend on it. My guess is that you want Tom and the others to trust you with the architectural idea, but it keeps getting distorted through their lens. What if you took the time to show them how having a real technical architect could propel their own vision further? What if they could see what you see?"

His eyes wander while he thinks about this. I wait to see if he has any questions.

After a moment, I decide to ask a question that has been on my mind for a few weeks. "Ever consider that you might care too much what the CEO thinks of you?"

He laughs. "Yes, I need him to make me permanent CIO!"

"That might be what's getting in the way."

He touches his moustache carefully and asks, "How so?"

"When we need validation from others, it can communicate a lack of self-confidence."

He brings his hand to his cheek and squints at me, which I interpret as disagreement. I try to clarify what I mean. "When they think that this is more about *you* rather than about them, they can't hear you."

"What am I supposed to do about that?" His voice rises an octave, and I can sense the frustration.

I'm sympathetic. I appreciate his confusion. "Here's how I look at it. You want to build trust and be seen as a leader within the organization, not just within IT, correct?"

He nods and crosses his arms across his chest. We're in a vulnerable spot for him, and I fight the impulse to also close my body. I remind myself that our bodies are having a conversation and that I want my body language to match what I'm saying. "One of the criticisms that you got in your 360 review was that your peers think that you're arrogant and uncollaborative, right?"

He nods calmly, but he's still squeezing his chest tightly. This is really tough territory for him.

"The thing is that you aren't arrogant, it's just how they are receiving you. When they don't understand what you're saying, they feel insecure. They think that you think you're better than they are."

He unfolds his arms and touches his nose with his index finger, which is an indication that we've hit on something else he feels insecure about. "I always feel as though I'm having to prove that I know what I'm talking about. And you're telling me that I'm making them feel insecure?"

"That's my guess."

What I love about working with Sandeep is that once he makes these connections, he's able to see the implications.

Now he offers another example: "Is that what happened the other day as well? I was in a meeting with Larry and the CFO. They were asking me to review a couple of major initiatives that my predecessor started before he left. These are big, expensive projects that are taking a long time and that are tied to a lot of promises…" He pauses, turns towards me as though sharing a secret and says, "I have my doubts."

"What kind of doubts?"

He pushes his hands into his pockets and looks down at the ground, as though he were a student reporting to a teacher. "This is the problem. The former CIO was so good at telling people what they wanted to hear. Expectations are not aligned." He continues to stare at the table, his hands hidden from view.

I decide to just ask him the question: "Can you tell me what you're feeling right now?"

He scans the cafeteria. "I feel like people are going to be really disappointed with these projects."

"You think these projects are a mistake?"

He looks in pain. "No, no. Not exactly. I just think that the expectations are not…" again he pauses to search for words. "Entirely accurate, let's say. And I tried to talk about my concerns in last week's meeting, but maybe Larry couldn't see it through this lens?" He swallows his voice, and I can hear him struggling with something. "He kept asking me if I believed in my team, which of course I do. My team isn't the problem. The scope is the problem."

I nod and think about all that we've been talking about: lenses, perceptions, understanding, confusion. Then it occurs to me: "Sandeep, how do you feel about conflict?"

He smiles a half-smile and leans back in the booth. "I hate it."

CHAPTER 3

How do you feel about conflict?

The cafeteria is empty now, and Sandeep and I begin the long walk back to his office to finish our session. The IT Department is stashed in the back of the building overlooking the parking lot, suiting most of the staff just fine. As much as Sandeep wants to be seen as a leader within the company, he has to fight the urge to hide at his computer. I see him struggle to keep his head up in the hall and to make eye contact with people as we walk through.

When we get to a sunny part of the hallway where we can see the woods that border the parking lot, I turn to him. "What do you hate most about conflict?"

"Conflict is fine with me if it's with my team. I can be direct with them. Something happens to me when I need to manage up." He shoves his hands back into his pockets and his presence shrinks.

Something feels off though, and I can see that his hands are balled into fists. "Do you think that you might feel angry as well?"

He looks up at me, surprised and takes a step back. "What do you mean, *angry*?"

"It's just a guess, but is that maybe one of the feelings you have when you have to manage up?"

He touches his cheek, and then looks up at the ceiling before turning back to me. "Why would I be angry?"

That's a good question. I can think of lots of reasons why someone might feel flustered or upset at their boss. Only Sandeep knows this answer. Whenever I notice a lot of body "chatter" like this, I think that there's probably something going on under the surface.

"I don't know," I say, "but there's something here. Tell me more about what it is about conflict that you don't like."

We start walking again, and he settles into a less hurried gait. "I suppose that some of it is the way I was brought up. In my family you don't question your elders. I want to be seen as a good team player." His tone is flat, which belies the tension I sense under the surface.

"I've seen you in meetings say no to things that others have requested. What's different about those moments?"

He opens the door to his office and lets me in. It's set up more like a war room with monitors and various readouts of how the systems are doing all over the company. It's pretty distracting to me, but I know that he feels comfortable in here.

We each take one of the vinyl chairs near the larger monitor, and he says, "I don't mind saying no or pushing back if I think that they're asking for something that puts other priorities of the company in danger. I guess I don't see that as conflict."

"Okay, then what do you feel is conflict?"

He touches his moustache. "I feel embarrassed for them."

"Embarrassed about what?"

He smiles and rolls his eyes. "So many things: the fact that they believed what the previous CIO told them, the fact that he told them those things, the fact that I have to be the one to tell them the truth. The previous CIO told them that they would save time and money through efficiency. That was a lie. If anything, we will have to spend more money and be less efficient."

And *there's* the anger.

It's always amazing to me how our emotions will interrupt whatever we are saying and, like a selfish actor, upstage whatever we thought we were going to say. If you try to suppress your emotions, they will almost always find a way to steal the scene, and in this case there's a darkness that comes over his face as he talks.

Usually, whenever I hear anger in someone's voice, I try to consider what they might be afraid of. Fear and hurt are usually right under the surface of most anger, but they are difficult to get to directly. "Sandeep, can you tell me what you *wanted* them to hear in that moment?"

He folds his arms and gazes intently on a corner of the room, away from me. He doesn't like this question. "That they're making a mistake. Reality won't bend just because promises were made." He takes a big breath and holds it. When he speaks again, his voice comes out hoarse and emotional. "I've never failed anything in my life, but I can't see a way through this. We're going to let everyone down."

He leans forward in his chair and rubs his head. His eyes are a little bleary and red, but I get a sense that he's also a little relieved to have said it out loud.

"How do you feel now?" I ask, not wanting him to stay in that dejected place for too long.

He sits up and offers a half-smile, "I guess I feel lighter, but I don't understand why. I said basically the same thing a minute ago."

"Maybe, but what I heard this time was less about them or the projects and more about how you feel about the situation. Am I right in thinking that you're a little angry at the former CIO?"

He smiles tightly and nods.

"So why not just say that?"

He gives another embarrassed smile and rubs the back of his neck in frustration.

"I know that others on the leadership team liked him and didn't want him to leave. I feel like I'd be disappointing them, talking behind his back and not being a team player." He rubs his forehead. "I told you I don't like conflict."

"Maybe the conflict is mostly internal. What if they are more open to that criticism than you realize? Try this, *what do you want them to hear?*"

His eyes flick to the screen to check something that turned red for a moment and then green. He puts his fingers together in a steeple shape and looks up at the ceiling before saying with confidence, "I want them to hear that this project will cost more money than it will save, by a factor of ten."

It's always fascinating to me how words sound so much clearer when we are able to separation our inner emotions from the message.

"Yes, that's much clearer. They can't see what you see, Sandeep. This is the problem with most things in life. You have knowledge that they don't have, but it's being muddied by your inner emotions, and probably exacerbated by their own. What if you could share your lens with them in a way that helped them put down their defenses?"

"How do I do that?"

CHAPTER 4

Can you put your ego aside?

t's the stuff of all advice columns, self-help books and daytime talk show psychologists: life gets easier if you drop your ego from the equation. Good advice, but it often leaves out an important question: How do I do that? How do I recognize that my ego is in the way and once I've recognized it, how do I get rid of it?

I've figured out that there are two questions that help people put aside their egos in a situation (if they are willing). These questions have become the two pillars of all my work. My holy grail:

The first is *What is the big picture?*

The second is *What if it weren't about me at all?*

I stand up at the small whiteboard in Sandeep's office and draw two stick figures for him and an empty square between them to symbolize the topic that they are trying to resolve.

"Let's look at this objectively," I gesture to the stick figures, indicating which one is Sandeep and which one represents the CFO. "This conflict isn't about you, and it isn't about him. It's not about the former CIO at all. This is about what's best for the company, right?"

Sandeep nods.

"Great." I point to the empty square. "Let's try this again, what do you want them to hear?"

He's taking notes in a small journal now, carefully copying the diagram on the board and he looks up to answer. "That I need them to trust me."

There's that *need* again. "Go back to what you said a few minutes ago and take all the need out of it this time. Remember that this isn't about you."

There's something fascinating that happens to people when they become aware of words like "need" of "should" in their vocabulary. There's this light that comes into their eyes as they realize their unconscious habits.

"Okay," he says, leaning his body towards the board while that "light" comes into his eyes, "I want them to hear that we're going down the wrong road."

"And?"

He stands up to point at something that only he can see on the whiteboard, and when he speaks his voice comes across clear and strong: "And no matter how far you are down that road, it's always less expensive to turn back than to keep going."

Now we're onto something.

"Can you offer any specifics? Try this, 'What I know about this technology is...' and see where it takes you."

He steps back from the wall and crosses his arms. Rather than seeming defensive, this body language feels to me more like a deepening of his thinking. Sometimes we cross our arms like this just to signal to the other person that we need a little bit of space while we figure it out.

I take the hint and lean back on my heels and stay quiet.

"What I know about this technology," he says, "is that while it does promise to automate a lot of processes, it requires us to use their system of categorizing and retrieval. It's like hiring someone to rearrange everything in your kitchen. It creates an unnecessary dependency." He stops to think about this analogy for a moment, then shakes his head and chuckles. "Actually, it's worse than that. They reorganize everything to fit their system and then they charge you a ransom each month to tell you where they put everything. Imagine paying someone each month for the right to use your own toaster!"

He spreads his palms open and shrugs. We both smile as we realize the absurdity of this example. His face is open and calm for the first time today. Now, let's see if he can bring it home.

"That's well put, Sandeep. You might have to go into more detail than this with the Executive team, but the analogy makes sense given what we've talked about in the past. Now, tell me why *you* don't want to do this project."

"I thought that you said to take to the ego out of it?"

"By that I mean take the "need" to be seen and heard as "important." We still want to hear your perspective. We want to understand your 'so what'."

He touches his mustache with his fingers again as he looks into the middle space between us and searches for the words. I resist trying to rescue him. After a few moments he looks up at me. "It makes me mad when companies just go for new technology that doesn't make them better. I'd still use COBOL over Python if I thought it fit the task and gave us a better chance at success."

He's comparing the older computer language from the 1950s (COBOL) to the relatively new and popular programming language that was invented in 1990s, which many new programmers use (Python).

"That's excellent, Sandeep. You've just made a great argument for the team to listen to you and trust you."

He leans his back against the whiteboard and seems both relieved and perplexed. "How so?"

"By speaking your truth, clarifying your analogy, and not making it about your ego, you've shown them just how much you care about practicality. I can't imagine what's more like-minded for an executive team of an insurance company than a CIO who cares more about practical application than new technology."

"So, I just tell them all that and you think that will work?"

"Well, I think that if you can tell them what you just told me and take away the need to be understood, you will give them the best chance to hear you. In the end, that's the best we can hope for."

Taming the wolf:

How can you manage tensions and miscommunication in the workplace and be trusted more?

First, don't take things personally. But as we'd seen in each story here, it's difficult to remember not to take things personally, even in the best of circumstances, so don't get down on yourself if you forget.

Second, learn how to communicate better through conflict.

Third, remind yourself that most of the time it isn't about you at all. It's about how you're being perceived.

Whenever I find myself in conflict with others, I try to figure out how I'm making this about me (*I want to be right, I want it to be my way, I want to be understood*) and then I see what happens when I let that refrain go. I remind myself that I can always pick these thoughts back up if I need them later.

Try thinking about the next conflict you are in as an experiment in real time: how would it change the tenor and feeling of the conversation if I didn't need to be right? What would happen if I were more interested in listening than I was in telling? What if we could arrive at the same conclusion regardless of whether I could take the credit?

Most people would like to avoid conflict on the job. I don't blame them. Conflict is uncomfortable, and I don't mean the kind of conflict where people are shouting names at each other and threatening to "take it outside." That's beyond conflict; that's war. I mean the kind of subtle and ever-present conflict that arises in collaboration. Our ability to navigate this type of conflict allows us to not only cooperate more, but also to be more creative.

Allow for differences. Just try it. It's hard. But try it. We don't learn and we can't grow if we only hold onto safety and comfort. The less personal we make it, the less about you it is and your need to be "right," the easier it is for people to hear what you're saying.

Part 4 — Bianca

"Words are sent actively with content. You must listen for the intent of the words in order to receive them, giving the words meaning not only from their intention, but from your own point of view and expectation."

—UTA HAGEN

How do you project confidence?

The curse of knowledge is a real thing for people with deep technical background. For them it can be impossible to discern which things are the most important for their audience. This is especially true in high-pressure situations. The irony of people who struggle with the curse of knowledge is that they can appear to others as not listening, not being prepared, or giving too much information. They might miss the question entirely.

For a few years early in my career, I worked with pharmaceutical companies preparing for FDA Advisory Council Hearings. My role was simply to work with the scientists, doctors, and statisticians on how they told the story of the data. These stories were rarely straightforward. Having so many smart people in the room could make things even more confusing. In this story, you see what can happen when you're willing to get centered, listen carefully to the question, and trust your own intuition.

Robert, the CEO of a mid-sized, rare-disease pharmaceutical company leans his elbow against the railing and asks the question everyone around him is thinking, "Can anything be done about Bianca?" The lobby of the Hilton at Logan Airport in Boston is chilly, and I stand with my arms crossed waiting as Robert's gaze lands on each of us in the circle. He lets the question hang in the air.

I'm here with three other colleagues, all consultants hired to help this pharmaceutical company navigate the challenges of an FDA Independent Advisory Committee hearing that is only a mere six weeks away. They all turn to look at me. Usually, these sidebar meetings are about strategy and tactics, which means I can stay silent, but the CEO's question about Bianca is really for the communication coach, me.

Bianca is in trouble. She's the one responsible for making the clear case to the FDA about the efficacy of the company's new drug. So far, all she's done with her practice presentation is to create confusion and doubt.

"She has to have more confidence!" Robert puts his finger on my shoulder, and for a moment I can feel his fear (masquerading as disapproval) reverberate through me, and my stomach clenches. I nod and unfurl my arms so as not to appear defensive (and to try to settle my nervous system). Just then Jane, my colleague and lead facilitator for the training, steps into the circle and speaks up.

"Maybe she's just the wrong person for the job. Do we have anyone else who can do it?" Jane is tactical by nature and good at keeping things moving, so I understand her desire to act quickly. She's quick to pull a speaker who can't deliver, and in cases like this, we usually don't agree.

The CEO shakes his head, looks down at his phone which starts buzzing in his hand. He mutters, "See what you can do" as he breaks away from the group to take the call. It's a classic non-answer to Jane's question and she's visibly annoyed.

As I watch him walk away, I try to remind myself that everyone here is afraid, and that fear is the thief of confidence. I turn to Jane with as much encouragement as I can muster, "She'll be fine!" but she rolls her eyes at what must sound like weak bravado. I don't blame her skepticism, I've only been doing this for a year, and I'm still considered the "new kid" on the block, but I believe in the formula I am experimenting with to help any person transcend their obstacles and be heard.

It starts here: there's no one "perfect" way to present ideas or data. There are ways to do it clearer, simpler, and better, but I've learned not to judge the presenter's effectiveness by how they look or sound.

Second, it's not just about communicating what you know. It's about communicating what you understand and why in a way that people can *receive*.

Third, if you want to build trust with your audience, you must trust yourself.

I judge a presentation (and the presenter) as successful when it's able to bring together context, knowledge and feeling in *such a way that allows for the audience to connect with the speaker and the message.*

I am confident that Bianca, who is warm, engaging, and coherent, can deliver on all of these principles. Who knows, she might even be great. I walk up to the ballroom where the rest of the team is waiting to continue the mock hearing. I'm thinking about what I've learned about Bianca so far: she's originally from Italy but speaks perfect English with only a slight accent, having studied and lived in the States since she was a teenager. She's a smart and relatively younger member of the team, but she doesn't appear intimidated by the work at all. With her combination PhD and MD, she brings a deep understanding of the science and the potential impact for the new drug. Even so, she's had a few shaky moments at the microphone over the last few months, and the more senior executives of the company have been quick to question her abilities, which has shaken her confidence.

In the last few days, I watched her get stuck in a negative feedback loop. As her confidence has dwindled, she's been putting more pressure on herself, trying harder to "get it right," which in turn makes her look and sound shaky. The executives see the shakiness and put even more pressure on her, and the cycle continues. We need to break this pattern if she's got any chance of staying at the microphone. There's a sense of panic among the team, and Bianca is becoming increasingly isolated because of it.

It's time for a coaching session. I step into the "breakout" room across from the main ballroom. Bianca is huddled over her computer at the table in here, surrounded by paper copies of her presentation. I can see that she's working on her slides. She looks up at me and frowns. "Ahh. I forgot that we were meeting now. Cavolo! (A common Italian exclamation, which literally means *cabbage.*) One minute." She writes another sticky note for the slide people before closing her computer.

I ignore the feeling that I'm intruding and sit down in one of the several black, vinyl roller chairs arranged around the table. Often bland and featureless, this room has a few nice touches: plastic daisies on the table and a print of a New England farm on the wall. "Rough morning, huh?"

Her shoulders stiffen, and she frowns again. It was a rough morning for everyone, actually. Nobody escaped criticism, but she took the brunt of the Chief Medical Officer's tirade today. He never mentioned her by name, but it was obvious in his takedown of the whole efficacy strategy. Bianca was stoic throughout the whole thing, nodding and taking notes, but the negative impact on her was clear.

"It was fine." She brushes away some hair from her eyes and with it some of the emotion from this morning. "I'm working on fixing the slides."

I've watched people in this situation before: they cling to the idea that all they need to do is make the slides clearer, that data tighter, and it will solve everything.

"Bianca," I say as gently as I can, "let's talk about the presentation and the Q&A."

She nods her head absently. "I just have to find the error in the calculations that Dr. Nee mentioned this morning. I can't believe that I didn't see it." Her voice sounds raspy and tired.

I take a deep breath to let out some tension in the room. These days are stressful, and we're all breathing shallowly. That thinness in her voice is most likely the stress of holding her breath while working.

"Do you want to talk about what happened during the Q&A?" I'm trying to be casual, but I can feel the CEO's finger on my shoulder and the weight of expectation in the practice room across the hall. I remind myself for the hundredth time already today that this isn't about me.

It wasn't just that Bianca stumbled through her slide data earlier this morning. It was how the first question of the mock hearing took her by surprise. After ten minutes of talking and calling up five different backup slides, the question was still left unanswered.

She shakes her head now and angrily clicks something on her computer. "I was so stupid. I totally missed his question."

In reality, she panicked and gripped the podium like the room had tilted sideways. Then she interrupted the questioner twice in an attempt to answer before he even finished (which, incidentally, just served to annoy the questioner and make him more aggressive). The fact that she brought up a series of slides that had nothing to do with the actual question didn't help much either. Again, to her credit, she didn't fall apart.

"What do you think happened in there?"

She swings around to look at me. "I *knew* the answer to that question. I wrote the description in the briefing book that we sent to the FDA." Shaking her head and pulling her body up straighter she says, "I just need to work harder."

"Well, what if that's part of the problem?" I chance a smile, but she isn't having any of it. Outside the window I can see a desert of concrete and the occasional airplane taking off.

"I can't understand it. It is like I just went blank." She shakes her head at me and peeks back at the slides up on her screen. I can tell that she wants to snuggle into the comfort of working on the data, but we're going to have to deal with this instead.

"Bianca," I ask. "Have you ever heard of the term 'the curse of knowledge'?"

CHAPTER 2

How do you choose what's most important?

The more you know about a topic or subject, the more that knowledge can become a curse when trying to answer simple questions. You may ask yourself which details are the "right" ones? How much do your interlocuters need to know? Do you just dump it all on the table and hope that they figure it out?

To be persuasive, you need to understand how to bring the *right* details and to provide the context for those details. It requires you to think not only about what you're saying, but also about how it will be received. Besides, what good is knowing the right answer if nobody can understand you?

"The problem," I tell Bianca. "Is that you're thinking about too many things at once. You're being *too* smart for the moment and it's making it confusing."

She waves away the compliment with a smirk. "Not smart enough, obviously."

I turn in the chair so that I'm facing her. The HVAC system above us stops and the room is suddenly quiet. I can't be certain, but I sense something shift in the way that she's listening. "I'm being serious. When someone asks you a question about the data, you have to sift through a lot of information and context. I imagine that you're thinking about all the ways you could answer, right?"

"Sure." She shrugs.

"And it's really hard to know which answer *is the answer* they want, right?"

"It shouldn't be."

"Maybe, but I think that we make it harder by making it so complicated."

She pulls herself up in her chair and leans towards me. For the first time since we first started working together, I have her full attention.

"What do you mean? How am I making it complicated?"

"By *trying* too hard."

She searches my face for a moment to see if I'm kidding. I stay neutral as possible. "You're making fun," she says finally. "The whole point of practicing is to try harder."

"The point of practice is to get experience answering the questions. The goal is to ultimately make it look and feel effortless."

She shakes her head. "You don't understand scientific inquiry. This isn't a tea party; it is a real scientific debate. We have to know what we are talking about."

Her voice rises and the pressure she's feeling starts to show through the cracks. I don't want to make it worse, so I lean back in my chair and give her some space before I say with a smile, "I agree, this isn't a tea party." Just then the HVAC kicks back on, and I'm conscious of having to raise my voice over the thrum. "But in this setting *how* you answer is almost as important as *what* your answer is."

"How so?"

"These hearings are like an old Hollywood movie. There are the good guys and the bad guys. The FDA, mostly because it's their hearing, are almost always the good guys. That makes you and your team the villains. The more at ease and genuine you are, the clearer your answers are, the less likely they are to put you in that role."

There's another flash of anger and she shakes her head. "That's ridiculous. We've devoted our whole lives trying to alleviate the impact of this genetic defect in these kids. I can tell you personally that the patients and their families don't think we're the villain."

I nod in agreement. "The problem is that *trying harder* is about bringing more effort. This means tension. That extra tension in our body and your voice can unintentionally confirm their bias."

She looks out the window at a plane taking off and sighs. "Okay, okay. *How* I say things matters. What does that have to do with 'making it more complicated'?"

Perfect.

I make some space between me and the table to illustrate my point. "Okay. Notice how you feel physically right now in this conversation. You got it?"

She gives me an uncertain nod. I push my chair up against the table, leaning my body and my stomach into the hard edge of the table. I strain to keep that pressure consistent and ask her, "Do you notice any difference in how you feel now?"

She lets out a sweet, relaxed laugh. "That looks so uncomfortable! I wouldn't want to keep talking with you like this."

I smile, push away from the table, and say, "You already know more about the efficacy of this drug than most people in your company. The pressure that you're putting on yourself, even though it's internal, makes you and the audience uncomfortable. It brings unnecessary tension to the moment, just like me pushing into the table with my body does."

She presses her fingers together in front of her lips as she reflects on this idea. After a moment she leans forward, places her elbows on the table and asks, "What does this have to do with being the villain?"

"It's all about the tension that we bring to the moment. Tension is often read as defensiveness, or it can even antagonize. Add a sense of fragility or uncertainty to it, and the audience will feel a strong aversion."

"I'm not fragile!"

I know this, but her defensive tone isn't going to help her convince anyone. I choose to let it go and instead get us focused on next steps.

"Of course, but this is about perception. Imagine for a moment that you're watching someone walk a tightrope. It's a dangerous profession, but tightrope walkers all try to make their movements seem casual and effortless. The more effortless they make it, the easier it is for the audience to enjoy the danger. The goal is to make walking the tightrope or answering questions at the microphone seem like a walk in the park."

"But it's not! It's so hard." She laughs and sweeps a lock of hair back behind her ears.

"It's incredibly hard, but we can't look to the panel or the audience to understand that. Do you remember yesterday when that consultant who used to work for the FDA asked you that weird question about the mechanism of the drug?"

She groans a sound of recognition. "That was so awful. I just didn't hear the question. I was so focused on bringing up all those slides we worked on the day before."

"Let's watch the video." I reach to get my computer.

"Oh God no!"

I click on the video. "We'll do it without the sound on, okay? I want you to see something."

Together we watch her walk up to the microphone in the ballroom and grip the podium tightly. She's nodding and looking down at her notes, but there's a tension in her jaw. I freeze the video right as she's calling for her first slide. "What do you see?"

"That I look like I'm about to throw up?"

I laugh. "Okay, but what do you notice about your body language?"

"I look like I'm holding onto the podium for dear life."

"Exactly!" I start the video again, and this time I run it faster, and the jerky motions mimic old silent movies.

"I'm swaying back and forth. And why do I look like I'm mad at the questioner?"

"Do you remember what you were thinking right at this moment?"

"Not exactly." She closes her eyes for a moment, remembering the feeling. "I was thinking, *don't screw this up.*"

I jump up in a pantomime of excitement. "Exactly!"

"So what? *That* can't be the reason I got the question wrong. I mean I just didn't hear it."

"How could you possibly hear it when you were so busy beating yourself up?"

She sighs and pulls at the cuff of her shirt. "I feel like we're trying to undo decades of behaviors in one hour."

"Not undo them, just bring awareness to them." I touch the knot on my tie to check that it's straight and then laugh at my own behavior. "Look, we have these old habits because they worked for us at some point. I touch my tie, some people clear their throat, others clench their jaws. Who knows, maybe it helped you get through Med school, you know?"

Laughter and a nod. This is good.

"But it won't work in this setting," I say. "The more pressure we put on ourselves internally, the harder it is to stay present. When we aren't present, we miss the question *and the questioner.*"

"The questioner?"

"Yes. He asked a terrible, rambling question. He was actually asking you for help, but you missed it. You couldn't hear him or see him because you were so focused on getting it right. When you're relaxed and feeling confident, then you can think clearer and focus more on the what's being asked. We can ask for clarification, but we often don't. Do you know what most people are thinking when they ask their questions?"

"What?"

"They are thinking about themselves."

She smiles, "Okay, then what do I do with that?"

"Take the pressure off of yourself. This isn't about you, it's about them. It's about the question itself."

"All right, but what *do* I do?

"You get curious."

CHAPTER 3

What does it mean to be curious?

When I think back to my early twenties and my first years of teaching, I'm painfully aware just how defensive I was. Teenagers have an uncanny sense of uncertainty in adults, which can make standing in front of them uncomfortable. It took me awhile to stop trying to tell them things and instead just listen and be curious. What are they hearing? What are they thinking?

It often helps to just get curious. What are you hearing? How are you reacting? Where is there confusion? Curiosity is one of the greatest tools to connecting in a more present and meaningful way. The problem is that we have to let go of the illusion that we're in control.

"Curious about what?" Bianca asks as she points her feet in towards each other under her chair.

"Well, let's start with body language. When you asked your question, did you notice that your feet changed position?"

"Did they?" There's a little lilt in her voice, and she looks down at her feet, as if surprised that they are a part of the conversation. "What does that mean?"

"Depends. Can you remember what you were thinking just before you shifted?"

The light from outside the window suddenly gets brighter and warms up the table. She glances at the window and then at me, "I was feeling uncertain how this was going to help. I guess I was thinking that I would never figure this out."

"Perfect. Thank you."

"Is that bad?"

"It's neither good nor bad, but it does have unintended consequences. When I do this, what do you notice?" I focus on a negative thought and let my face and body respond naturally.

She leans back to look at me. "It looks like you're angry."

"Yeah, that's about right. It's just my inner dialogue leaking out in my body and face."

"So, don't leak?"

I laugh. "Not if you can help it. Recognize that your inner thoughts might have outer expressions." I open up the video again and show her a still of herself frowning in the middle of question. "The more curious we are about what's happening to us, the easier it is to notice what we're communicating. This frown was not about the questioner, right?"

"That's right, I was trying to remember which slide to call up."

"But can you see how it might look like you're mad at the questioner?"

Bianca purses her lips and swallows as she stares at the screen, trying to reconcile what she felt in the moment with what the video is telling her. This is the good and the bad about video. It shows us how people see us, which can sometimes be in direct opposition to how we feel about ourselves.

Breaking her gaze from the video, she looks at me and asks, "What can anyone do about this? I wasn't feeling annoyed with him, I was annoyed with myself."

Bingo.

"That's the problem. Being annoyed with yourself just *looks* like annoyance, disappointment, or anger *at* the other person. Not only is self-punishment unhelpful; it makes things worse. We can be a little gentler with ourselves."

There's this moment in every coaching session where you can see the client come up against the wolf, or the thing that they've been afraid to face. Sometimes, when they are in the right place, rather than run away they drop all their defenses and surrender. This is when real change happens, when we let go of the need to protect ourselves and instead just connect. I watch as Bianca takes in this idea of being gentler with herself and I sense that something shifts.

I give us both a minute to settle into this new feeling. She reaches into her bag for a bottle of water and says with a hint of sarcasm, "Less self-judgment would be nice."

"It's possible. Breathing more can help."

She laughs. "My trainer is always telling me to breathe."

"Well, we tend to hold our breath when we're putting in more effort. We hold our breath and put pressure on ourselves, but that makes it hard to stay present and *hear* the question."

She closes her eyes and nods.

I say, "Maybe the key skill here is listening rather than answering. Listening is less about effort and more about staying present in the moment, physically and mentally. Besides, if you don't understand the question, you can always ask for clarification. You might get a better question. You'll be surprised."

I can see her head start to spin. She's nodding absently while folding up her computer and putting her papers back in her bag. I know they're expecting us back in the ball room for more practice, so I go for broke.

"Bianca, you know more about this drug and the disease than almost anyone in that room. The goal is to listen, connect and communicate from a place of self-trust. Do you believe you are the right person to answer these questions?"

She stands up, lifts the bag to her shoulder and says defiantly, "Yes, I do." For the first time today, I hear the confidence in her voice.

"Then trust. Stay present in the moment, listen to the question and the questioner, and above all else, trust yourself. You do that, and you give the story a chance to be heard."

CHAPTER 4

What if you got out of your own way?

"Could I have slide 52 please?" Bianca's voice is a little shaky, but no one seems to notice as they're waiting for the new data slide to appear on the projection screen.

The experts at the long table across from her are all flipping through their briefing book to prepare their next questions. I catch her eye as she looks out over the panel, and I take an exaggerated breath and mime planting my feet firmly on the ground.

She smiles, adjusts her stance, and then lets out a deep breath. The next question she gets is a straightforward one about the pre-clinical data, and she does a solid job walking everyone through the results. She spends a little too long on the slide, however, and I can see a number of people on the panel touch the button on their microphones, eager to get to their question.

Then one of the experts, a statistician, asks a rambling question about two deaths the company had in an overseas clinical trial. Everyone in this ballroom has known that this question was coming, and yet we all feel the tension in the room ramp up when it finally arrives. I'm sitting behind Jane, and she whispers something to the CMO who shakes his head.

Bianca says, "I want to make sure that I fully understood the question Doctor Fullman, are you asking specifically about the cause of those deaths or are you asking for more details about those international facilities?"

Doctor Fullman looks back at his notes. "I'd like to know more about the deaths themselves. How do you know that they weren't caused by interaction with your drug?"

Bianca nods and calls for a backup slide that shows the mechanism of the drug and how it is supposed to interact with the nervous system. She begins to walk us through the story again of what they saw in the preclinical trials before she is interrupted by Doctor Fullman. "That's all well and good in your slide, but the whole point of doing a *clinical* trial is to prove out whether what we find in preclinical translates to actual practice. Two deaths are suspicious in my mind. It's hard not to think that they're related."

I can tell that Bianca is momentarily stunned by his directness. Then the Moderator, who's running the Q&A for the company, touches her shoulder to indicate that he can answer this question. But rather than relinquish, Bianca just shakes her head in a bewildered way and says as if as an aside, "But there's almost no way that *both* deaths could be the result of the drug."

"And *why* do you think that is? Pray, enlighten us." Doctor Fullman is usually professional, but he can also be a sarcastic jerk when he feels he has a good crowd. It's not looking good for Bianca.

She scans her notes and then starts again in a clear and measured voice, "Well, when I looked deeper into the files, it turns out that one of those patients was in a terrible car accident. The medical examiner just listed him as having died while on clinical trial. Of course, we can't rule out anything one hundred percent…"

There was a stunned silence in the room, before Doctor Fullman said, "Is this true? The patient died from injuries sustained in a car crash?"

"Yes sir," Bianca says.

"And the other patient?"

"Complications from pneumonia, which is not unusual for this disease, but as I said, we recognize that we can't entirely rule out any connection with our drug."

Doctor Fullman studies the slide before clearing his throat and turning to look at the CMO. "Well Robert, I think that you have found out a way to talk about the deaths." He looks back at Bianca. "Well done, Doctor Potenza, let's take a break."

Bianca smiles and walks away from the lectern as the din of conversation grows in the room. I catch up with her near the coffee table. "Nice work up there. What did you notice?"

She looks around the room, then whispers, "I was thinking about what you said that I know more about this data than most of the people here. I felt so unsure of myself, I mean why didn't anyone catch this before? But I figured that the facts were the facts, and I decided to just get out of their way and let them speak for themselves."

Taming the wolf:

I know that it's easy to say, "trust yourself" and harder to put it into practice. When we signal that we don't belong (think of Bianca's tendency to sway or her frowning at herself), we give people the impression that we *don't* trust ourselves, which causes a negative feedback loop.

Unfortunately, we develop habits, both verbal and behavioral, that confuse our message. These habits may have worked in the past, but they will not help you reach the next level in your communication.

Here's something that you can try: be still, breathe easily, and keep your face neutral. This will help you stop signaling and eventually, once you become used to the feeling, you will present with more confidence.

The negative thoughts might not stop, but *you* can stop feeding them. Notice how Bianca softened when she realized that the pressure she put on herself was causing her to frown, which in turn made her look defensive?

We can be convinced that our self-criticism is somehow helpful, but it gets in the way of our ability to connect with the audience. It throws a shadow on our face and disconnects us from the other person. Stay curious, focus on the question rather than on the problem, and redirect that self-criticism towards connection.

Knowing a lot of information is only part of the challenge. Choosing what information is the most helpful to the audience and boiling it down is the harder task. Curiosity will help you with this, as will patience.

Be curious about what you *understand* about a topic. Rather than trying to convince people of a position, try to think of it instead as sharing your perspective. Think as well about your audience's perspective.

Lastly, ask yourself the question: "What would I need to know to understand this idea, if I had never confronted this information before?" This simple lens swap will help you be better at choosing what details are the most helpful. It also keeps you in a conversation, which is more engaging and helpful to the listener.

Part 5 — Drew

"Behind the need to communicate is the need to share.

Behind the need to share is the need to be understood"

—LEO ROSTEN

Are you creating dissonance?

Anyone who feels a sense of ambition and a need to be liked will notice the complicated story Drew tells of himself. He can be supremely confident in one setting and full of insecurity in another. In my experience most of us are like Drew, but many are better at hiding it than he is. In Drew, I hope you will see the profound change that can happen for someone when they are willing to get honest.

The air-conditioning is turned way up to offset the Austin heat in July, and I secretly wish I had brought a sweater. There are ten of us sitting in a circle in a cramped conference room of a small downtown hotel, finishing up the last hour of an executive workshop with a software company. I'm here to work with the whole team, but I've also been asked to observe Drew, the newest member to the team.

The vinyl banquet chairs squeak noticeably whenever anyone moves, and we try to stay still while the last speaker, Charlie the Chief Financial Officer, stands to tell his personal story. I think we're exhausted from the long day, but I am still riveted as he tells us the story of the night that he and his wife brought their adopted baby-daughter home from Russia. His voice is thick with emotion, and he rubs his eyes with the palm of his hand. Much like many other members of this team, Charlie usually has a sharp, sarcastic wit and a rough exterior. But he softens as he talks about his joy mixed with terror on that night, fourteen years ago. Everyone in the room is leaning forward in their chairs now, except for Drew who is sitting back with his arms crossed. There's an expression on his face that I find familiar, but I can't quite place it, except that it makes it look as though he's the judge of this talk.

When Charlie is done speaking, the silence in the room feels reverent, like a church service. I ask teams like this to share personal stories for several reasons: to build connection, to feel what it's like to be more vulnerable, and to cultivate trust. I finally break the silence and say, "Thank you so much Charlie. We appreciate you sharing such a personal story. It's five thirty now, and it's been a great day. I want to take a moment now to reflect on everything we've heard. Anyone willing to start?"

This kind of question can be a risk with a group like this that isn't used to sharing personal stories. It's not often that business leaders are asked to emote while at work. The CEO, a tall, thin man in his fifties named John, shoots me a concerned look, and reaches down by his feet for the agenda. That's when Drew speaks. He's a general manager for the whole product division in the company that serves supply chain businesses, which means he's responsible for 80% of the bottom line. He's somewhere in his late-twenties or early-thirties, tall, at least 6'4", and might be mistaken for a slender Viking. Right now, he's sitting on his hands like a child expecting to be chastised.

"I'm grateful to John," he pauses to clear his throat, "for, uh, giving us this time and I want to thank everyone for their stories."

I feel the room tighten, and a pained look crosses his face.

What's going on?

"In retrospect," Drew's voice gets louder here, maybe to push through his own nerves, "I could have taken more, uh, risks today."

There's silence again, but it feels tight, like everyone is waiting for it to end. People start to fidget in their chairs. Drew turns to the Chief Human Resources Officer, a dark-haired, woman named Leslie. "Leslie," he says, "I was most struck by your share about having to take care of your parents when they were dying."

Leslie stiffens but manages a tight smile and whispered, "Thank you."

The CEO looks down at his shoes again and starts to rub his neck. Both are signs that he ought to see, but for some reason he doesn't read them. Drew looks at his hands and smiles again as he relaxes a little. He throws his hands out to the group, but his eyes don't focus on anyone in particular. They just gaze over everyone's heads. "Guys, what can we take away from this day to keep us closer?"

Now I see it. It's as though he were simultaneously taking control of the group and asking for permission to be in control. It's not going over well with the rest of the team. His question is one that I also wanted to ask the group, but it's too late now. I try to think of a way to carefully wrap up the day when someone jumps in. The COO (Chief Organization Officer), a short, burly man who was uncomfortable from the start and has been making defensive jokes all morning, finally blurts out, "One takeaway is, don't borrow Drew's running shorts!"

Everybody breaks out in laughter and starts to pack up. Some are laughing awkwardly about Drew's story earlier this morning in which he shared about a time that he soiled his shorts while running in his first marathon. I appreciated his courage to share that story with the team, but as his face reddens and he grimaces at the laughter, I can tell that he feels hurt. I make a move to try to pull the group back to Drew's question, but they're done and already making their way to dinner. Drew walks out of the room alone.

*

The next morning John, the CEO, and I meet for breakfast in the hotel restaurant. He tucks his napkin neatly into his collared shirt and points behind himself in the general direction of yesterday. "What did you think of Drew during the workshop?"

I take a sip of water, trying to sort through my own feelings, settling finally on an observation. "Well, he hasn't exactly integrated himself into the group."

"No, but they don't *hate* him." John rolls his coffee mug between his palms and raises his eyebrows as if to ask, "do they?"

"I think he makes them uncomfortable." I recall the expression on Drew's face when everyone was laughing. "And I think they make him uncomfortable as well."

John brushes away a crumb from the table and shakes his head. "They respect his ability. He turned around a failing product in less than a year, increased growth, and doubled our profit. He's an amazing leader." On the word leader, he slaps his hand on the table.

"He is? How so?" I don't mean to sound so surprised, but it's hard to imagine that we're talking about the same awkward person I saw in the meeting.

"He cares about people and his team knows it. He remembers people's birthdays and sends them cards. He listens to them and looks them in the eyes. Most importantly, he never second-guesses himself or his team. The last GM created a mess, even though the Executive team liked him." John's voice trails off, and I get the sense that there might be some self-recrimination here. "Look, I need Drew to figure this out. We need his voice on the team."

"He seems young. Maybe he just needs some time?"

"We don't have it. This market is changing, and we have to start changing with it if we want to grow. People are pushing back. Drew just gets it. He's the kind of leader we have to become." John picks up his fork, gesturing towards me with the handle. "I want you to work with him. Get him to be more of a presence in that room. Teach him how to get followership. If he can do it with his team, then he can do it with his peers."

Our eggs are placed in front of us, and John digs in.

"Okay," I say, "but only if he's got a long runway. I don't want to work with him if he needs to turn it around in a month."

"If he is willing to work with you," John says, "then I'm willing to give him time to figure it out. We don't have forever, but we've got enough."

What's humbling about trying to be humble?

A month later I'm walking through the company's main building in Austin, Texas with Drew as my guide. The place is enormous for a company only about five-years-old. His division alone has over two hundred employees. He makes a point of having conversations with almost everyone we pass in the carpet-lined hallways. Their faces light up when he talks to them, and his questions appear genuine. When we get to our meeting room, he says, "This actually used to be the former GM's office, but I had it converted to a meeting room."

I take in the big picture-windows and the gorgeous view of the skyline and the river. "Why did you give it up?"

He shrugs. "I've been advocating that we deconstruct some of the old symbols of hierarchy in the company. The rest of the Executive Team is resisting. They say they need the privacy. I get where they're coming from, but privacy often can look like elitism." He shoves his hands deep into his pockets and suddenly seems small.

Behind him on the wall is a quote from Gandhi that's been neatly framed. Drew follows my gaze and reads out loud: "'Be the change you want to see in the world' is a motto that I try to live by." He crosses his arms and takes a wider stance with his legs. "I follow the principles of the servant leader, and I never take credit for myself."

I never take credit for myself.

I agree with the principle, but I'm struck by the irony within any statement that boasts about not taking credit. I feel a little annoyed, and I decide that this is a good enough place to dig in. "Drew," I say. "Humility seems important to you. Can you tell me a little bit about what it means to you?"

He plops down in a chair across from me and stretches his long legs out in front. "Humility is about always thinking of others first and yourself last."

I feel resistance build inside me again, which probably comes from the word *always*. I get the sense that he's trying to prove to me how evolved he is, which is actually doing the opposite. I decide to poke at it.

"Sometimes we have to help ourselves first, right? Like oxygen masks on airplanes? They tell us to put our masks on first before helping others?"

He nods slowly and tucks his feet under his chair, signaling an inner uncertainty. It's fascinating to see how he see-saws his presence between being large or small. His body is having a lot of confusing conversations with the world.

"Maybe," he says, "but that's not what I mean when I think of leadership

I press harder, "Do you remember that old saying, 'the captain must go down with his ship?'"

He springs forward in his chair. "Absolutely. That's how I see leadership. A good Captain always goes down with his ship."

"Why is that?" I recognize that I'm being provocative with this question, but I'm curious what's in his mind. It's a delicate balance between provoking and being curious. When I manage it poorly, it just leads to an argument. I'm not sure which one this will be.

"Well, I often think about Edward Smith, the captain of the Titanic. He chose to go down with his ship." He rests his chin on his fist, and after a moment he says, "I love historical figures, as you can see."

"Yes, it's helpful to look to history." I take a breath and begin to recognize just how hard Drew is trying to come across "leaderly." I'm beginning to realize that my showing up or "my being here" is not necessarily something he's psyched about. "I wonder though," and I try to create as much space and generosity as I can, "if he could have gotten everyone off the boat safely, should he still have gone down with the ship?"

He crosses his legs, and a shadow of annoyance flutters across his face. Despite my attempts at being open, he didn't like being challenged. "I don't follow you."

I open my palms on the table so as to keep my body language non-threatening. "I have this theory that some leadership principles can become reductive, and therefore counterproductive. You seem to pride yourself on taking a low status position with your teams."

He nods and recrosses his legs back towards me. I take it to mean, *I'm listening.*

"I don't know about 'low status'," he says, "but I do make sure that everyone knows they are more important than I am in the big scheme of things."

"Yes, which might be great with your team, but I wonder if it's causing some confusion with your peers. In a way, you might be signaling to them that you're low-status, yet taking a high-status position. Does that make sense?"

He folds his arms across his chest and shrugs. I point to his chest and ask, "Do you mind telling me what you're feeling?"

He looks down at his arms folded across his chest and says, "This just feels more comfortable," and shrugs.

Oh boy. This is not going great.

"If it's okay with you, I want to show you what I see."

He nods, and I copy his posture in my chair, making sure to also mimic the way that his eyebrows knit together like he's disapproving of something.

"Do I look relaxed?" I ask, making sure to giving him a smiling wink.

He smiles back, and something inside of him uncoils as he sits back in his chair. "Okay, maybe it doesn't look relaxed, but I feel more natural like this," indicating his arms. This is good. If he's willing to take feedback like this, then anything is possible.

"Well, I'm not going to argue with you about that, but I want you to know that you don't present as someone *natural* right now. You look like someone who's defended."

"I'm not feeling defensive," and his voice cracks a little on the words, which almost would be funny if he weren't so unaware.

"Did you notice that?" I point to my throat.

He shakes his head. "Notice what?"

"That cracking sound on the word "defensive"? Also, look at where your hands are."

"I think maybe I just had an itch."

I remember how vulnerable it feels to have someone point out what your body is doing and tell myself to go slowly. "You're partly right, I'm sure," I say, "but let's make space for the possibility that you also could be having an internal reaction to this conversation."

"I'm not feeling defensive if that's what you mean." His body stiffens.

It's funny, and this time I laugh out loud. "You do realize that '*I'm not feeling defensive*' is kind of defensive?"

To his credit, he lets out a chuckle and shrugs. I decide to try again.

"Drew, let me ask you a question. How do you feel about the Executive Team?"

He shoots a quick glance at the door behind me. "Well, it's clear they don't think much of me."

"Why is that?"

"I think in part it's that I'm so different. My father was in the military, and I grew up always moving, always adapting to new situations. Most of this team struggles with change and feels threatened. . ." He trails off, distracted by some thought. I see his hand go back to his neck and wonder if there's something vulnerable about this that I don't see.

"So, the issue is that you're different?"

"No, that isn't what I mean." He lets out a sigh of frustration. "We have different ideas about leadership. They want to be in control, and I want to give away control." A darkness passes over his face when he mentions control, which gives me the signal I was looking for.

"Drew, do you think that you might be angry at them?"

He lets out a surprised chuckle, "What? No. I mean if I'm angry with anyone, it's myself. I don't get angry at other people."

I smile gently and say, "There's a pretty good chance that you might be lying to yourself about that."

What's my body saying?

Most of us are unaware that our bodies are speaking all the time. I remember being in a workshop with the great improvisation teacher, Keith Johnstone, who all afternoon pointed to people's body language in the class to show how they were communicating the opposite of what they were saying. Someone tried to play low- status in a scene, but they kept taking high-status physical postures. Their body betrayed the fact that they felt superior, even though they were trying to act inferior. It was fascinating, but it also felt like we were all stripped naked that day.

Since then, I have tried to pay attention not just to my own body language, but to the body language of others. One thing has become clear to me in that time: communication is so difficult in part because we don't know what's happening to our bodies. The hope is to get curious and just notice our body language without judgment. What am I doing right now? What am I feeling? What is the message I'm sending?

Drew recrosses his legs and rubs the back of his neck. "I don't know what you mean. I'm not angry at anyone." He pauses and rubs the back of his head. "I might feel a little frustrated with myself, but that doesn't mean that I think I'm better than they are."

Bingo. He thinks he's better than they are.

"Drew, maybe you're giving that message unintentionally. In a sense you might be telling the team that you think they're beneath you."

"How so?"

"Look, John asked you to help him change the culture in the organization, right?"

"Sort of." He flexes his foot so that it points straight up. "But I know that I'm the junior member on the team, so…"

"That!" I point to his foot, and we both lean around the table to get a look at it pointing straight up.

"What? Am I doing something wrong?"

I shrug. "Not wrong, but I noticed your foot flex just as you were talking about your relationship to the team."

He tucks his foot back under his chair and looks back at me, "What does it mean?"

"I don't know, but in my experience, it could be a reaction to something happening internally. What emotion were you feeling then?"

"I'm not sure. It wasn't anger."

One thing that I've noticed is when people say *it's not* ____,
there's a good chance it might be _____. "Maybe not, but there's
definitely something happening."

"I don't…" He trails off, straightening out his foot and pulling
himself up in his seat and smiles. "I feel a little self-conscious."

I nod and can identify with that feeling. "I get that. Sometimes
it helps if we can be curious and non-judgmental with ourselves.
Our bodies are always talking, so what might they be saying?"

I stand up and step away from the table, and motion for him to
stand up with me, which he does, but with a sense of caution.

"Okay," I say. "Now try leaving your arms at your sides and
your feet firmly planted on the ground."

He follows the instructions, but his eyes signal some distress.

"This is essentially a neutral state," I say. "Everything else
that happens in your posture is in reaction to something either
internal or external. So, from this place see if you can notice anything weird that your body does. For example," I cross one foot
in front of the other and shove my hands in my pockets. "What
do you notice?"

"That's weird. Your whole presence shrunk."

"Exactly. I call these contractions. It's as if we were contracting
our presence from the room."

I gesture for us to sit back down. Then I point at his foot. "Take
that moment when your foot was pointing straight up."

We both look at the offending foot, which rests innocently on
the floor.

He says, "What does it mean that I flexed my foot like that?"

"I don't know what it means, but whatever was happening was not in your awareness. And the unconscious body language talks as loudly as your voice."

"And that's the goal, right? Be more aware?"

"Exactly."

How do you deal with your emotions?

"Okay, so what do I do with this?" Drew says. "Will it help to earn the Executive Team's trust?"

We're walking back through the hallway on our way to get something to eat from the cafeteria now, and I'm struck again by how different Drew is in public spaces. He's so confident. It isn't an act; he exudes a warmth to everyone he sees.

"Well, let's start with this idea of trust," I say. "Why would they trust you?"

We're at the deli-counter making sandwiches when he's interrupted by two workers who call out his name. He asks them about their kids and a toothache that the older woman, Dora, had been complaining about recently. He grabs his sandwich and an apple and turns to me, beaming. "Because all I want to do is help."

"That's great, but we're terrible at reading other people's intentions. Especially when the body language seems to contradict that."

"And you're saying that my body language stinks?" He takes a bite of his apple and smiles. He's much more relaxed, and I get the sense that he's not competing with me anymore.

"No. I'm saying that your body language is telling them a different story than you intend. It communicates a contradiction between what you're saying and feeling, and that's a problem."

We sit down in one of the booths at the end of the room. It's quiet in here. We are way past lunchtime, and the afternoon sunlight streams in behind us and warms the air in spite of the air conditioner. Drew seems much more relaxed in this space, and I offer him a piece of my cookie.

He shakes his head no and gestures with the apple towards his sandwich, indicating that was enough.

I draw a circle in the air with the cookie. "What just happened?

"What do you mean?"

"What just happened between us?"

He looks at the cookie and then at me and says, "you offered me a piece of your cookie, but I said no thanks, I'm good."

"Yes, but we didn't speak a word."

Drew laughs, shaking his head. "I don't know. We just understood each other."

"And that's what we want in our communication, right? It's almost like dancing. Our bodies are talking to each other all the time, you know? Every time I move, your body wants to answer back. In this case, our bodies and our intentions were totally in sync and led to an understanding."

He looks thoughtfully at the cookie and then asks, "So what do you think is happening when I communicate in the Executive Team meetings?"

"I'm guessing that it has something to do with how you feel about them and how you think they feel about you."

"I just want them to trust me."

I nod sympathetically. "Is it working?"

He shakes his head and takes a big bite of his apple.

"Let me ask you, do you trust them?"

He stops chewing for a moment, swallows and asks, "How so?"

"Do you trust them in the way that you want them to trust you?"

He seems confused by the question, so I try a different way to ask the question. "For example, do you feel about them the same way that you feel about your direct reports?"

He lets out a sigh. "Probably not." He squints to look out the window behind me, and a feeling of sadness passes across his face. "I feel left out. I try so hard to be vulnerable with them, but I'm always on the outside. I don't get it."

And there we go.

"Sometimes we use vulnerability as a defense mechanism," I say. "You may try to communicate openness with your words, but your body language signals defensiveness."

Drew studies the apple in his hand. "How am I defensive?"

"Well, sometimes we feel defensive when we think we will be judged. Did you notice that there were a few times today when you felt defensive with me?"

He nods uncertainly. "Okay. So, just stop feeling defensive?"

"Well, it's not that easy. You have to first understand *what* you're defending."

He places his apple core onto a napkin and rubs his hands together saying, "I think that they don't respect me. When I'm with them, I feel…" he hesitates, placing his hand on his chest, "*unsure* of myself."

I nod and think about how unfairly I've characterized Drew this whole time. John was right, his willingness to be honest and vulnerable is remarkable. The problem is that he can't be vulnerable *and* defensive. It doesn't work to build trust.

"Drew, trying to be vulnerable from that place is dissonant. It's like saying, *here, let me show you my heart, but only if you promise not to hurt me.* In places of power, like an Executive Team, that behavior invites confusion at best, aversion and distrust at worst."

"Wow," Drew says softly, leaning back in his booth.

"Yes. Wow," I say.

There are these moments in our lives when we get real feedback about how we're perceived. A good friend, counselor, manager, teacher, or coach can give you feedback that can forever change how you see yourself in the world. It's a deflating experience to recognize that you're not necessarily who you think you are, but it is also a moment of real self-actualization.

Only when we're willing to see ourselves and our behaviors clearly do we have any chance to change. For those of us who choose to accept the feedback, our lives are changed forever. This is what I see in Drew's eyes as he leans forward and asks, "So, what can I do about it?"

"For starters, stop trying to prove to the team that you belong. Trust yourself. You have something valuable to offer them, beyond platitudes and philosophies. Be yourself in that room. Treat them like partners."

For a moment his eyes drift off, trying to puzzle through something far away. "What if I can't change?"

"This isn't easy stuff, but the more you think of them as equals, worthy of your trust, the easier it will be to trust them. They're not bad actors, and John wants you there. Quiet the judgments and the doubts, and your body language will quiet enough for them to see you."

We sit for a few minutes in the silence. Uncertainty shadows Drew's face. I finally offer the only true thing I know to say to anyone: "The truth is, this will be the hardest and simplest thing you've ever done. Drop the mask and all the different ways that you defend yourself, and you will find that you're already there. When we stop trying to show that we belong, people are finally able to accept us for who we are."

Taming the wolf:

Most of us don't pay any attention to what our body is doing. But if you notice that you're contracting (hugging yourself, tucking feet under your chair, sitting on your hands), be curious about what might be going on inside of you. Yes, you might be cold, but you also might be having a feeling. Our bodies tend to react to feelings and thoughts unconsciously. If your body is doing something without your permission, it makes sense to pay attention.

One way to tell if there's something going on is to take a neutral posture and see what happens. For example, if I'm feeling agitated or upset, I can't hold a neutral position for long. I will feel the agitation grow inside me. The more aware you are about your body, the more likely you will be able to settle it down and avoid creating a sense of dissonance like Drew did in the meeting.

Sometimes just the thought that we *should* belong somewhere can create a tension and an unease in our presence. Check-in with your thoughts and postures; see if you can detect what's behind them. Is this a judging thought? Is it negative about myself or about the people in the room? How is this thought affecting my presence and connection?

Try not to rationalize the thought (i.e., I'm thinking negatively about Bob because he didn't approve my project), rather focus on whether it's a helpful thought. Drew's assumptions that he wasn't trusted and that he couldn't trust created dissonance with his eagerness to please and show that he was one of them. Clearing those create opportunities to connect and influence others.

Part 6 — Carol

What's your big idea?

I t used to be that everyone had at least one good book in them, but now I sense that we also feel that we have at least one good TED talk. I spent the first four years or so of my career working with Maine's TEDx, and I had the privilege of coaching some amazing people. Each one, much like Carol whom you'll meet below, would come in with multiple messages they wanted to get across. The coaching work was often around prioritizing those ideas and finding the one, big idea that grounded everything. It was also about helping people see a path to being more vulnerable with their audience.

"I feel inspired." Carol says as she strolls into my office and scans the room for a place to put her stuff. She plops a tote bag full of books and notes onto the couch and gently lays a kayak paddle against the wall. She is in her mid-thirties, with a bright smile, red curly hair, and big, electric energy that seems to resonate almost from her skin. Her clothing tends to be a mixture of the practical and the whimsical, and today she's actually wearing a lifejacket and some sort of waterproof top along with a bright neon sunhat. She's leaving our meeting early today to go kayaking in the bay, and I get the impression that she's in a rush to get out of here.

When she and I talked on the phone a month ago, she shared that she feels reluctant about a local TED talk she's been asked to do. She's made a name for herself over the years as an enthusiastic outdoors guru, a kind of "thought leader" of the outdoors, and she's become a minor celebrity. She published a "self-help" book on the restorative power of nature last summer, which increased her brand. She's also been an entrepreneur, a community organizer, and pretty much a superstar in every way. She's frustrated by this this Tedx talk, however, and that frustration is now spilling over to me.

"I can't believe you're making me do this without notes and in sixteen minutes. It's impossible!" Her tone is all defiance and hurt as she sits down across from me.

The TEDx format can catch speakers by surprise, not just the "no notes" rule but also the strict allotment of time. I've noticed how people feel compelled to cram everything into their talks. It's difficult not to feel the pressure to follow in the footsteps of Brené Brown or Simon Sinek, speakers who exploded into fame in their first talks. A well-received TED talk can launch a career. In my experience that much expectation can paralyze people, and I'm seeing some of that in Carol.

"Those are the rules, Carol. You know that."

But she's already moved on, shaking her head and picking up her notebook. "I've also decided that I'm *not* giving another talk on the evils of technology." Her tone is aggressive, but I can see that she feels cornered. It's hard to choose a path when, like Carol, all you see are the traps.

In these coaching sessions, I try to listen for people's "big idea." The TED program insists on this simplicity, but in my experience simple is not easy. What I often hear is a hodge-podge of ideas, combined to satisfy some imaginary checklist that people have about these things. Ask someone to focus on one idea, and they tell you why they can't. I try to just invite them to boil their ideas down. It can sometimes feel to both of us like we're in a fight. This one, thankfully, I see coming. I ask Carol, "So, what do you want the talk to be about then?"

She blinks at me a few times and then pushes her point harder. "You see, technology actually makes going out into the wilderness easier."

I can feel the tension as she speaks. The next few minutes are going to be crucial to establishing trust between us. Carol made it clear originally that she didn't really need a coach, but I was assigned to her anyways. Few people like help that they didn't ask for, and this has already put our coaching relationship in a precarious place.

"That's a refreshing take," I say, hoping that I sound agreeable. "Let me ask you, what's the one thing you want the audience to *feel* after your talk?"

"Feel?" More blinking. I wonder if she's nervous or if this is just a habit for her.

"Yeah, what would you like them to be feeling when they leave?"

Carol takes off her hat and gives it a look of annoyance before putting it down on the floor and rubbing her hair. "I guess I want them to feel inspired?"

I'm impressed. Most people struggle to identify what they want their audience to feel, but Carol went right there.

"Hey, that's a great goal. Here's the problem, you can't inspire by focusing on what you don't want them to hear. That's just going to confuse your audience."

She shakes her head and crosses her legs. "No, no, you don't understand."

I resist the impulse to also cross my legs, knowing that the more open I can be the better chance we have at connecting. "Here's how I look at this. We get this small window of opportunity to be heard and capture an audience's attention. When we bring up the things that we *don't* want them to think or believe, it muddies the waters. It makes the communication messy."

"I don't follow." She makes a show of looking at her watch as she says this.

Uh oh. I'm failing at my own advice.

"Well, you may have heard of this, it's an old mind game. Tell me what pops into your mind after I say this." I pause for effect, and then spread my hands wide like a magician doing a trick and say, "Don't think of elephants!"

There's a sudden rush of warmth between us as she smiles and says, "I'm thinking of elephants…"

"And that's why we don't want to waste any time focusing on what we don't want them to hear. Be disciplined about what you *do* want them to feel and hear instead." I hear myself emphasize the "do" a little harder than I mean to. I realize too late that she's defensive again, and this is exactly what I'm counseling against.

As if on cue, she stiffens and crosses her legs away from me. "I *don't* want to give the same outdoorsy talk everyone gives." She flips the pages of her notebook, and a mixture of sadness and frustration comes into her voice. "I want this to be special."

"I hear that." I try to think of how to help her stop comparing her talk to others and focus instead on what she wants to say. "And I believe it will, *if* you're willing to trust your own story."

Are you bringing the gold?

I reach across the conference table from Carol and grab a fake gold bar that I use as a prop. "Let's pretend for a moment that this is a real gold bar, okay?"

Carol lowers her notebook and gives the bar a curious look.

"We might disagree on how much that bar of gold is worth in dollars," I say, "or whether philosophically it *should* have value in our society, but nobody in our culture will question that it has *value*, correct?"

"Sure." I notice the ambivalence, but I choose to ignore it. It's probably just the uncertainty of where we're headed with this.

One of the things that I see happening with TED speakers is that they can feel pressured to present themselves to the audience as someone important. All that effort tends to be an obstacle to communicating their authenticity and insights. Asking people to validate your importance will only invite suspicion and distrust.

When presenters bury the value that they're offering under an avalanche of words, jargon, and hand waving, all it conveys is a lack of trust (both of the audience and of the speaker herself). I want Carol to see how she could start from a place of trust, which would allow her to present her message without explanation or defense.

"Any talking I did to convince you of the bar's value would just confuse things. Like, if I said to you, *this is definitely not a fake bar of gold*, what would you think?"

She laughs a deep belly laugh, which I have come to understand as a kind of release of tension whenever we become aware. "Okay. Yes, I get it."

"I think that we underestimate our own value, our *gold* if you will. We do too much, I don't know, preamble maybe? Explaining? I wonder if sometimes we are unclear what the actionable value is of what we're saying. It's like carrying a gold brick around and thinking of it as a paperweight."

Her fingers trace the outline of the gold bar, and she picks it up in her hands and holds it over the table. "So, essentially you're saying that I need to trust that what I'm offering has value?"

"Yes, as long as we understand the value of the offer."

I reflect to myself on how important it is to value ourselves as messengers. When we try to prove our value to others, we make it so difficult for anyone to trust us.

"But I need to establish myself as an authority, don't I? I need to prove that I belong there, right?" She places the gold bar back onto the table, crosses her legs again, bouncing one foot in the air.

I note the urgency behind the words "need" and "prove." It's so much like what an actor feels when preparing for an audition. *I need to get this part to prove that I'm good enough.*

"Maybe," I say, "but in my opinion a good talk happens when you allow yourself to stand in front of the audience, naked from all defensiveness. We can't ask for trust *and* for assurances that we will be safe."

I pause again to let her think.

She stops bouncing her foot and turns to look out the window. "What do you mean by naked?"

"Well, I was just thinking about acting. Sir John Gielgud once said 'acting is half shame, half glory. Shame at exhibiting yourself, glory when you can forget yourself.' I think that when we put down our defenses and allow ourselves to be seen, we forget ourselves. It's a generous act of courage."

Carol is still holding her lifejacket in one arm and lets it slide to the floor. One layer of armor gone. She then asks, "What does that look like?"

I try to think of a good example before turning it back to her. "Do you have a favorite teacher?"

She smiles and leans her head to one side, enjoying some memory. "That's easy. Mrs. Huntington in the fourth grade. She had this knack for getting me to try things I was sure I couldn't do. She taught us Shakespeare for goodness sakes! I didn't know it was supposed to be hard until we read it again in eighth grade." Her gaze moves from some middle space between us, directly to me. "She was like that. How do I get there?"

"Well, let's start with your big idea." I point to her notebook. "How many ideas do you have written down there?"

She looks down and flips through them. "Twelve, but they're all important and related." While her words are defensive, her tone is less so and I get the sense that she's beginning to soften.

"Okay, but what if you could only pick one? Which one would you choose?" I decide to add for extra effect, "Remember that you want them to feel inspired."

She goes internal and gives me a vacant stare, which either means that she's thinking or that she's shutting down.

On an impulse I add, "What do you want your audience to experience with nature?"

Something about this question snaps her back into focus and she starts talking. "I want them to lose themselves in it, to appreciate the power of nature in themselves, to *feel* their bodies and spirits in this world. It changed my life, and I know it will change theirs."

While she talks, her voice is strong, but the tone is soft and there's a sense of connection and spaciousness between us.

I wait for a moment before speaking.

"That." I point to my chest, "That's it, Carol, I could feel that. Now, can you prove it to me?"

As soon as I say the word *prove*, I regret it.

A worried crease forms on her forehead as she flips open her notebook. "Well, all the current research indicates that the brain prefers to be in nature. There are these studies that show how having nature, any nature at all, can make our minds more vibrant. Some studies even show that just walking in the woods for fifteen minutes will lower people's blood pressure, and that the psychological effects of being in the wilderness is enough to alleviate people's depressive moods or to even get teenagers to talk to their parents." I unfortunately pushed her up into her head and away from her feelings.

Time to pump the brakes. "Hang on Carol, that's a lot of great information, but what about the personal connection? The data is interesting, but it won't hold our attention. We need the story."

"What do you mean?"

"We want to hear why this is important to *you*."

"I don't want to make this about me." Her tone implies a condemnation of herself.

"I hear that," I say while leaning forward in my chair, "but people want to hear your story." I'm pushing too hard, I can tell, but I don't want to lose this moment.

She picks up her sunhat and begins to pick at a loose thread on the brim. "I don't like to talk about myself."

"I get that, but remember what we said about being vulnerable on stage? We want to see you be human."

She rips the loose thread from the hat with a sudden snap, then looks up at me. "I studied environmental science in college and my father was an avid outdoorsman. He used to take me fishing and hunting. The outdoors has been the only sane place in my life. Isn't that enough of a story?"

"What do you mean by sane? Tell us a little about your dad and about who he was to you. Let the audience in."

She looks at the thread between her fingers and flicks it to the floor. "But I lecture all the time."

"This is a general audience. You've got a chance to inspire people who might never have thought about the outdoors. Invite them into your worldview to see what you see."

I take a minute to see if this makes sense, and then I push a little further. "You want to share your worldview with them because you believe that their lives would be better off for it, right?"

"Absolutely."

"Then give them something more than just a lecture. Give them something of yourself."

She tosses her hat back on the floor. "Why should they care about *my* story? This is about nature, not about me."

Watching her shrink in her chair, I realize what's going on. She's scared.

"Carol, what scares you the most about this talk?"

What are you afraid of?

Carol's gray eyes focus on the middle space between us while she considers whether she wants to answer the question. Finally, she says, "I just don't want to make a fool of myself."

I identify so much with this fear. For so many of us, it isn't just the idea that we might fail, it's the idea that we might embarrass ourselves.

"I hear that." I nod in agreement. "What if you focused more on connecting with the audience rather than on avoiding being judged?"

"It's important to me that the talk be something memorable."

"Then you're going to have to be vulnerable."

Her eyes roll up into her head, and she audibly sighs. For a moment, she looks all of sixteen years old being told to stop slouching. "I *hate* that word. Everyone is always talking about being vulnerable, but I've spent my life proving that I'm not weak."

Ah. Now I think I see what's going on. "When most of us think of vulnerability, it's usually in this needy, *wounded* way that often makes us feel weak and defenseless. What if we were open without needing anyone to fix us or to take care of us?"

"Fix me?"

"Yes, it's like when someone starts talking and you get this impression that they really, really need you to like them. It's a turn off."

"That's it. That's what I'm afraid of. I don't want people to walk out of there and think, *she's just doing this for the attention.* That's why I want to stick to the facts, rather than share my personal story."

She checks her watch again, and I get up to pour her a glass of water. I can sense that we are close to something, and all this defensiveness is a smokescreen.

I try a new tact. "All the best speeches are a kind of story, aren't they? They're a mix of the personal and the universal. I'm just asking you to share a piece of yourself."

She nods takes a sip of water and says, "Honestly, I think I'm just afraid of falling apart up there."

There's *big emotion* behind what she's saying, but I can't figure out what it is.

"Could you try just telling me?" I try to sound inviting because I can feel her wanting to squirm away, and it seems to work well enough as she puts down her water glass and begins.

"When I was a kid, I always had trouble connecting with people. I felt alone all of the time even though I had three older sisters. My dad loved to hunt and fish, but the other three girls didn't have any interest in it. I tagged along with him whenever I could and learned to shoot and work with our hunting dogs. By the time I was fifteen I had done my first solo trip. Four days alone in the wilderness, hunting and fishing for my own food. It was honestly one of my happiest memories."

She pauses here and picks up her water glass again, staring into it. "He died while I was in college, colon cancer. One of his last good days was in the spring and we hiked out to our old deer stand, set up some chairs, and just listened to the sounds of the forest. In the spring the sounds are cacophonous and the whole forest feels like its crawling with life. He was in a lot of pain, but we didn't talk about the cancer at all that day. He told stories about growing up and his relationship with his father, which none of us had heard before. We didn't shoot anything that day, but it was bar none, the best hunting day of my life." She wipes her eyes with the back of her hand and says, "I miss him so much."

We sit in the quiet of the room and let the emotions ripple through us. It's a beautiful memory.

Then she chuckles. "See? This is a total downer. Nobody wants to hear my sad story."

"Nonsense, that's a beautiful story."

"But I don't want people to feel sorry for me, and I definitely don't want to cry."

"We can work on the crying part, but in terms of the audience feeling sorry for you, you're just going to have to trust them and trust yourself more."

"Well, how do I do that?"

CHAPTER 4

How do you become an invitation?

"Here," I say, breaking the emotional stillness of the moment. "Could you stand for a moment in the center of the room?"

Carol stands up, tucking her hands in her pockets.

I gesture to them and indicate that I want her to stand with her arms at her sides. She's uncomfortable, but she does it.

This is when we feel most naked, so I want her thinking about something else quickly. "Okay," I say, "now close your eyes and imagine yourself in the woods, some place specific and meaningful. Picture the smells and sounds."

She breathes in deeply, and her shoulders drop a bit as she smiles.

I'm impressed at how quickly she gets there. I can feel her tension leaving the room. She takes a few more breaths in and out, and then looks at me.

"Okay. I've got the place."

"Now imagine someone you love who you want to share this space with. Please don't pick anyone who will argue with you. We don't want to *convince*, rather we just want to share it. See if you can picture them here in this space with us."

She takes another breath and slowly nods her head. She starts to fold her arms across her chest and her lips pull downward into a frown.

"Okay, I don't know who you are thinking of right now, but that's not the person. Notice your body language. Can you feel the tension?"

"Yes. I was thinking of my sister, Ann."

"Yeah, we'll leave her out of this." I smile. "Who do you love to go on walks with in the woods?"

"My niece. She's only eleven, but she loves to go on hikes. It's like seeing the forest with new eyes."

"Excellent. Let's take your niece with you, then. Picture her here with you and imagine that you would like to invite her on a walk in the woods to this special, private place. Got it?"

"Yes." She takes another deep breath and her arms fall to her sides.

"Okay, what do you want to tell her about the woods?"

She smiles, and I feel something emotional start to well up inside me. I couldn't pinpoint exactly what the reason for the feeling is, but I'm certain that it's coming from Carol.

She says, "I would tell her about the smell of the spruce trees here in this forest. This is older growth, protected by conservationists years ago, and you can almost smell something deep and magical." She pauses. "I would tell her that this is what green would smell like if you could smell color, and that this smell and the coolness of the dark woods is what I think the word solitude means to me."

Tears are running down her face, and she pauses for a moment to wipe them away. "Jeez, I'm a regular faucet today."

I wipe the back of my hand across my eyes as well and say, "Carol, that was amazing. What a beautiful image."

"Yeah, well I don't think I will be talking about *that* at my TED talk."

"Why not? Or at least, why not allow yourself to go there?"

"Because it's scary!" She laughs as she shouts this and then puts her hands on her hips, "and because I'm afraid of looking stupid."

"It's not stupid. It's real. It's vulnerable. It's authentic." I walk around in a circle in a theatrical way, addressing a crowd of people who aren't there. "If you had to offer some data to back up the feeling that you just described, could you?"

"Absolutely. The bio-feedback research about nature's effect on our sense of well-being is remarkable."

"So, this would be a great place to put that in."

"Really? And you think people will connect to that?"

"Well, you still have a lot of work to do to shape the talk, but the heart of the talk will be that story about your dad and your niece. Your personal connection to nature is our gateway into the data."

"Ugh. I feel wrung out." She rubs her hands across her face and pulls her curly hair back into a short ponytail.

"It will feel that way for a bit, but the more that you practice from this place," I point to her heart "the easier it will get for you to access those emotions without feeling like you are losing control."

"So, is the goal to be emotional?"

"No. Emotion for the sake of emotion is just self-indulgence. For me the goal is to connect. When we can access our hearts, we can connect to other people's hearts. Through that connection, we build a relationship. The relationship connects us and changes us for the better. That's the payoff of being vulnerable."

She gives a wan smile and looks at her watch. "Okay, well I'm not going kayaking now, so let's get to work."

Taming the wolf:

We all have ways that we hide. Some might do it by decompensating, while others do it by being loud and assertive, but even that won't allow for a meaningful connection, unless you're willing to let down your guard a little and be seen.

When you are willing to be vulnerable, touch into those places that are personal for you, and share them with the audience, you give them a window into who you are. This in turn helps them see something in themselves. Genuine feeling is the key that unlocks people's imagination. For some, your courage to be seen can be a light in the darkness.

Much like the impulse that Carol had when she put her hands in her pockets after standing up, we want to hide anything from the audience that feels too revealing. An open stance can feel more generous and welcoming to the audience. In the same way, when you tell your story with grace, dignity and compassion, you offer the audience a generous way to absorb your information.

When telling a story, it's important to remember that you don't *need* the audience to take care of you. While it's crucial to be honest and vulnerable, don't feel as though you need to share things that are too personal or that make you feel fragile. Take care of yourself and your audience will appreciate you.

While Carol was sad, telling her story was not a traumatic experience. When we share a part of our selves to an audience, we let them in to a sacred space. Think of your stories as loving gifts to your audience and be generous in how you use them to share your ideas.

Part 7 — Alex

"We are tremendous people. We have tremendous things in us. We simply have to let ourselves be."

—CHOGYAM TRUNGPA

CHAPTER 1

What are your expectations?

've never met a leader who was good at what she did who didn't also doubt herself when trying to lead. I also find that the best parents are often the ones who talk about their struggles as a parent. If you're a leader, no matter if your organization is two people or ten thousand people, you can experience self-doubt and frustration at the same time. The trick is to avoid the trap of blaming those that work for you for the limitations you find in yourself.

How do you clarify your expectations with your team? How can you get better at peering into your blind spots? What is possible for your organization when you are willing to lead from a place of humility? Alex is a great example of how we can start.

At almost forty-years-old, Alex is no longer considered a young CEO in the world of tech. That being said, his voice sounds young on our Zoom call today, especially when he's agitated like this. While Alex often has a calm, flat demeanor, there's one thing that can really rile him up: incompetence in his team. Lately, his VP of Finance, Kevin, has been the source of frustration.

"Kevin's not going to make it." Alex says this as he settles into his home office. I can see that he's trying to stay measured, but he keeps tugging on his ear, which I've come to learn is a sign that he's agitated.

"What's up?" I ask, keeping my own voice casual. It's easy to get wound up on video calls when someone else is agitated, so I bring my awareness to my chair and open my palms up on the desk. I had to learn tricks to keep myself present while on video, and the more still and open my hands are, the better I can be.

"He's useless." Alex holds the "esssss" at the end of the word while he checks an incoming text. He's a little frenetic. A big part of what he and I do when we talk is to unpack his assumptions about what's really been happening at work, and this often feels like backtracking to him. "Kevin wants to go over his upcoming presentation to the board. I don't have the heart to tell him that I already put it together myself." Alex rubs his nose again with the palm of his hand.

I'd bet that Kevin is feeling nervous and wants Alex's validation. From the sounds of things, he's not going to get it. "It's that bad?"

"I'm starting to doubt that he can even add." He takes off his signature blue sportscoat and tosses it onto something just out of the video frame in a gesture of frustration.

I assume that Alex is being overly dramatic now. My understanding is that Kevin was a graduate of the Wharton School of Business and, while he's young, he worked a few years at Deloitte.

He's no dummy, and they hired him knowing that he'd have some growth to do. "What did Kevin do wrong?"

"In his first attempt, I found three errors in the first slide!"

"Maybe he was just nervous…" I realize mid-sentence how weak and defensive this sounds and trail off.

"It was an introductory slide!" He's shaking his head. One thing that's hard to ignore about Alex is how quick his mind is. He has one of those racing, far-ranging intellects. When he gives you his full attention, it can feel like laser beams on you. When he chooses to learn something, he masters it, quickly. If you're in an argument with him about the facts of a situation, chances are pretty good that you're going to be wrong. It's intimidating, but it also creates a blind spot for him. I'm beginning to understand that he's too quick to judge based on his emotional assumptions about people.

But I'm not going to argue with him right now. I decide to change tactics. "Okay, let's say that you fire him, then what?"

"I'll hire someone new. Someone better."

"Alex", I square up to the screen to increase my presence with the camera. "This may be Kevin's failing, but it's also an opportunity to look at your own behavior. You know that this is a blind spot." We've talked about this blind spot before. In fact, it was the main reason why Alex hired me.

I wait to see if I get any resistance, but he just smiles, lets out a deep breath, and nods. One thing that makes him endearing as a leader is that, despite his intensity (maybe even because of it), he's always willing to hear direct feedback. In fact, he craves it. This is another clue. I start in again. "Remind me again why you had to let go of Tom?"

Tom was their last product manager. There's a slight hesitation now before Alex answers, "Uh, he couldn't handle the scope of the projects. We needed someone with more experience."

"And your last executive administrator?"

He nods. "Well, I gave her plenty opportunities…" His words trail off and I wait to see if he will add anything. After a moment he just shrugs, so I jump in.

"Do you notice a pattern here?"

He tugs at his ear lobe and nods. "These were just the wrong hires. They weren't able to swim at the pace and depth that we needed."

I feel something tighten in my stomach. It's something about the "they can't cut it" argument. I recognize that doing a startup is hard, and that it takes extraordinary effort and talent, but I don't like putting all the blame on the person being fired. It's an easy way for Alex to avoid looking at himself.

"Alex, let me say those words back to you, and you tell me what you hear: *These were just the wrong hires.* What does that sound like?"

He looks off somewhere above the computer screen before saying, "It sounds as if I weren't involved in their hiring."

"Were you?"

"Yes."

I wait to hear if he wants to add more, but he chooses to stay quiet and stares back at the screen.

"And you hired Kevin as well, right?

"That's right, but it turns out that we need someone with more experience. He just can't handle the pace and the expectations."

I decide to take a risk. "Have you ever asked yourself how you might be making it harder for them to be successful?"

He nods, but I can tell by his half-smile that he doesn't agree. "How so? I've only tried to help him. I've been so nice!" His hand is on his chest as he says this to indicate sincerity, but I get the sense that it's defensive.

"Maybe." I shift in my seat and try to settle into my own discomfort. For someone who coaches others to communicate more clearly, I still struggle with conflict. I recognize that what I'm about to say will counter how Alex sees himself. "But it's possible that what you think of as being "nice" might *feel* intimidating and confusing to others. If I had to guess, I'd say that the problem is in how you give people feedback."

His fingers touch his throat as he considers this. Finally, he says, "Okay, I'll bite. What's wrong with how I give feedback?"

What kind of teacher are you?

There are a lot of reasons why someone may struggle at a new position in a company. Before we can give them feedback though, we must understand how we are looking at each person's struggles. It's difficult to help anyone if you believe that he/she is incompetent or unwilling. We have to get our own heads in the right place first.

"Before we talk about how you give feedback, I say to Alex, "let's make sure you're clear about what's happening with Kevin." I type out three options in the chat:

1. He can't do it.

2. He can do it, but he doesn't want to.

3. He can do it, he wants to do it, *but he doesn't know how.*

He reads these, then sits back in his chair, folds his arms and blinks slowly. When Alex's patience is thin like this, he goes still and quiet. I'm not so worried, because I know that he trusts me. The effect is disconcerting, nonetheless.

I say, "Ask yourself, which one of these have you been assuming was Kevin?"

The silence from his end continues, but I'm pretty sure I know which one he wants to pick. I can see by his eyes that he's making a show of reading the options and thinking. He probably senses a trap.

"The first," he says and quickly follows up with, "only because he's given me cause."

I can't help but smile a little at his certainty. "Okay, let's go with that. When you assume that he *can't* do it, then everything you say to him carries that message—it's a test of that assumption."

He squinches at me. "Like a self-fulfilling prophecy?"

"Pretty much. We tend to work to the level of expectation that our managers have of us. It's perverse, actually. If you *believe* that he can't, then it's almost as though it were his job to prove that you're right."

There's a lot more to say about the negative impact of this type of assumption, but I don't want to overwhelm him. For example, the assumption of incompetence is a fundamental lack of trust, which destroys confidence in young leaders. On top of that, once you lose that trust, it's almost impossible to win it back. It's better to begin every relationship with trust, than to start with distrust.

I watch Alex wrestle. "Okay, assuming that you're right about this, so what?"

Nodding, I sit back in my chair and spread my arms wide. "Think of this spectrum of possibility. On one side of the spectrum, he's incompetent, in the middle he's able but unwilling, and far on the other side, he's unsure how to be successful. Which one affords you and Kevin the most flexibility for success?"

He sits upright in his chair and thoughtfully pulls at his chin. Rather than answering my question, he says, "I guess I don't understand the difference between not knowing and *can't*. Aren't they the same?"

Sometimes questions are more like statements of belief, and this is definitely one of those times. For Alex, *not knowing* is tantamount to incompetence. I avoid the temptation to enter the debate and try to push past it. "Thinking that they are the same makes them the same. When you think that ignorance is the same as incompetence, you limit that person's ability to grow."

I look out my window and watch as big, white, puffy clouds slowly roll by. I want him to *see* Kevin differently. I turn back to the screen and ask, "He was a good student, yes?"

"Well, he did go to UPenn. You can interpret that how you want." Alex was a product of the University of California system and finds the Ivy League fascination out-East annoying. I decide to treat this as a yes.

"He was a good student then. We know he can meet expectations that are clearly defined for him."

"Look, it's his job to figure out what *I want*, not my job to spoon feed it to him."

There it is. In coaching just as in teaching, you're waiting for the other person to surface the obstacle that's keeping them from clarity. Often, it's what they believe about themselves and the world that prevents them from seeing past their assumptions. We don't realize how much our beliefs and thoughts weigh us down and keep us from meaningful change.

I can hear in Alex's frustration that he honestly believes his team should read his mind, and it's keeping him from seeing Kevin clearly. In the back of my mind, I sense that Alex is afraid he can't pull this off.

Alex is willing to reveal that what he's really upset about is that Kevin can't read his mind. It's an understandable, yet ridiculous expectation, which is why it's so important to say it aloud. We can hold the most ridiculous and self-damaging beliefs sacred, as long as we never have to admit to them openly.

What happens next on the Zoom is really important, so I stay focused on what I want him to hear from me rather than on trying to convince him of anything. And what I want him to hear is that this mind reading expectation of his has an impact on Kevin. Something is going on for Alex. It's as if he's afraid that he might be responsible for Kevin's struggles and wants to blame him instead.

"What if he thinks that you expect him to fail?" I pause to see if he reacts, but he doesn't reject the premise, so I continue. "It's really hard to trust yourself when your boss thinks you're stupid."

I wait for him to digest this. Alex can be judgmental about people, but he also has a huge heart. He quickly runs his fingers through his hair and then covers his mouth with his hand. I've noticed this gesture in people who recognize that they may have misspoken. When he speaks again, his voice is softer, more reflective, "He's not stupid. I just want him to be better at his job."

"Then you're going to have to start dealing with your fear."

How do you communicate what you want?

When I was a young teacher in my early twenties, I chose to direct Tom Stoppard's play *Rosencrantz and Guildenstern are Dead* as my first production. It's a monster of a play with complicated language, big philosophical ideas, and long, dense monologues. The actors were high schoolers, and they struggled a lot with the text. I tried to encourage them to believe in themselves and relax, but deep down I was panicking. I probably said to the actors, "Just relax and trust yourself" every rehearsal. The problem was that I kept thinking to myself that I'd bitten off more than I could chew.

What happened? First, even though I felt that I was speaking calmly to the kids, I was actually communicating frustration (as we've talked about, it doesn't matter if this frustration was with myself or with my actors). Second, my advice to "trust yourself" was useless. I might as well have said to the actors "be taller" for all the good it would do. How does anyone trust themselves when they believe that they are the problem? The more they struggled, the more fearful and tense I became. We were locked in this death spiral.

I couldn't help them trust themselves until I started to deal with my own fear. But what was I afraid of? In my mind, this play was a symbolic test. I felt like my own creativity and leadership was at stake. I needed the kids to trust themselves so that I didn't feel like a failure. My feelings and beliefs were getting in the way.

Perhaps Alex was experiencing something similar? Putting pressure on Kevin and others to be perfect, because of his own fear of failure. I ask him, "You've said in the past that everyone who works for you needs to know that you care about them. You've talked a lot about how a culture that is built on trust, equity, and excellence can do anything, right?"

Although he was trained as an engineer, Alex has deep respect for the psychology of teams and organizations. To him, trust is as valuable as expertise. Perhaps even more so since you can't go out and acquire it. He gives a nod with a thoughtful scratch of his chin. "Yes, that's true. But I don't get the fear part."

"Well, what if you're wrong? What if you can't build trust and also expect people to be perfect?" He needs to understand what's really at stake here. He can't be successful if he's always protecting himself from failure.

There's a moment of cool silence between us as Alex decides
how he wants to answer this question. He offers a half smile and
asks, "You don't think I'm wrong about culture and trust, do you?"

I shake my head. "No, but it's not a thing so much as it's a
quality of experience. It would be so much easier if people just
behaved in a way that allowed us to trust them, right?" He nods
slowly, but rubs the side of his neck, which tells me that he's
irritated by this question. I think I'm getting close.

I say, "Try this, what do you want *for* Kevin?"

His eyes brighten up and he leans into the camera a little with
his body, "*I want him to be better at his job!*"

While I can tell that the intent was to create an emphatic point,
what gets communicated instead is a sense of helplessness. "And
this," I say, "is where fear comes into play. I mean, it would be
easier to trust him if he didn't make any mistakes, wouldn't it?"

"Of course!"

"And that's what makes us feel out of control, you don't have
control of the outcome. As a leader of a company, your need for
perfection will only create a culture of mistrust and fear. In fact," I
move to open my body a little in the camera, "if we want to communicate trust, then we have to allow for mistakes, within reason.
We have to be willing to trust without proof." You must take the
risk to trust.

He looks at me with uncertainty, so I say, "Let's try this, what is
the major way that Kevin seems to fail at his job?"

He rubs his chin while he thinks about this, then leans back
in his chair and says, "What drives me crazy is that his mistakes
are unforced errors. Stupid mistakes like spelling errors or

miscalculations. He seems to want to impress me with the speed and volume of his work, but what matters to me most is the quality and purpose of the work. I want him to help me tell a better story with our finances." He stops as if tripped up by his own thoughts before saying in a tired voice, *"It's as if he were always trying to show me how much he can do, which ends up making me think he can't do anything."*

This. This is insightful. "It's as though he were trying to prove to you that he's trustworthy. Which is what you've been unknowingly asking him to do. This is how our fear creates problems. We put pressure on them to prove to us that they are trustworthy, which makes them tighten the screws too tight."

We're almost out of time, so I go for broke. "Do you really believe that culture and trust are going to be the keys to your company's success?"

He chews on this for a moment before answering, "Yes, I do, but it also includes something about execution. We can't have trust without credibility."

"Okay, then ask yourself this question, do you think that you could have the one without the other?"

The silence is hard to read at first, and I'm not sure if I made any sense, but then he nods slightly and says, "I guess I do. Or maybe that they are sequential. It feels like trust and credibility ought to come from competence. I don't understand why this is so hard for people."

I almost miss it, but I manage to catch the arrogance in this statement. He doesn't see that he's separating himself from other people, and that separation creates the message that he's "better than" they are.

"What if you saw your struggle with them as the mirror of their struggle with you? Just flip it?"

"What do you mean? See myself from their perspective?"

I nod. "Yes, think about how you started this whole conversation and how that experience might have felt to Kevin. Focus on whether your requests have been *credible*."

He looks confused. "I'm not sure what you mean by credible."

"Well, I think of credible as being synonymous with trustworthy. Ask yourself whether your requests were designed to engender trust, if they were trustworthy."

While he studies his notebook, I sit quietly. It's a meta moment for me, but I notice my own fear of wanting to walk him towards the conclusion that will make me feel like I'm right. A small part of me wonders if we ever stop needing to do this work.

After a minute he turns back to the screen with frustration, maybe with himself? "I think I've been setting him up."

I wait for him to go on.

"I thought I was giving him the space to show me what he can do, but when I look at it from his eyes, it must have felt like a trap." He clicks on something on his computer and says, "Here's an email I sent him a week ago: 'Hey Kevin, the board meeting is coming up soon. Put something together that will impress them with how we're spending our money. Use your judgment.' I mean, I was trying to sound light and casual, but when I think about it from his perspective, this must have been terrifying."

"Okay, so in what way are you contributing to a lack of trust?"

Many of us can get caught up in the *how did I not see this?* loop, but Alex isn't like that. Once he's aware of it, he only wants to focus on how to improve.

"Well, for one thing, I can see that what I thought of as empowering might be laziness on my part. I didn't want to explain what it was that I wanted."

"Good. How would you do it differently now?"

"Well, it strikes me that I don't really know how to explain what I want. I wasn't sure how to set up the slides until I sat down to do it." His hand goes back to covering his mouth, but I can see light shine through his eyes. He gets a strange pleasure out of finding ways that he can improve.

"This seems like a good place to begin. What if you used this as a reset moment with Kevin?"

His mind is still half on the slides, so it takes him a minute to hear the reset idea. "Reset, how?"

"I'd take this time to admit the tension and the feelings that have been going on between you and Kevin. Name them and name what you've been frustrated about and how your assumptions may have contributed to it."

His finger touches the buttons on his shirt. "You mean apologize?"

"Sort of. I mean identify the feelings in the air, admit your own part in it, then get clear what you want from him. Open the channel of communication. I think you'll be surprised by what you find."

He sighs and sits back in his chair. I can tell he's still frustrated, but he at least looks less angry. "Okay then. I'll give that a try."

"And remember to put the fear on the shelf. All you need to do is show up and open the channel."

He smiles broadly. "Right. I will leave my assumptions at home."

CHAPTER 4

What do you do with the fear of failure?

t's easy to offer advice on how to communicate with clarity, courage or compassion, but *doing it*, the actual changing of behaviors, is remarkably difficult. I've seen clients who were convinced that they were permanently stuck and by all accounts it looked like their situation was impossible. Somehow, many of them managed to change old behaviors, and beliefs about themselves, and the patterns that held them hostage.

They were willing to face the obstacle inside themselves and change their behaviors and their thoughts. In my experience, this change only comes when we're willing to step closer towards the thing that we secretly fear the most inside ourselves. Alex has been especially interesting to work with because he brings such intensity and willingness that I can track his growth in real time.

It's a beautiful, Maine summer day today, and I'm taking a walk along the Portland harbor, soaking in the sunshine and warm breeze. I get lost watching two tugboats guide a container ship through the harbor and almost don't notice the call from Alex. I pick up and duck into a sheltered area where the wind and noises from the harbor aren't as strong. Before I can even say hello, he starts talking: "I had no idea how scared he was," he says and pauses. He's in his car, and I can hear the Bluetooth-hiss of the highway. He follows up with, "and how scared he was making me feel."

It's not like Alex to talk about his emotions. "Hey Alex, great to hear from you," I say, just to get my bearings. "Tell me, how did it go?"

"Well, we had the reset meeting, and he was really forthcoming and pretty emotional. The problem was that the more he shared, the harder it was for me to stay present. I could feel myself shutting down."

"How so?" I try hard to concentrate. It isn't just all the background noise. Alex is also talking so fast. I try to imagine sitting across from him in a small room, and it helps me focus on being present. I've learned this tool from doing years of conference calls. Imagine yourself in the room with everyone else on the line and it changes the quality of your presence and your voice.

He clears his throat. "It's strange. I wanted to listen to him, but I also wanted to run out of the room. I vacillated between wanting to tell him that it was okay and wanting to tell him to stop talking."

I think about how vulnerable this last statement is. I have the urge to say something, but I wait.

Then he says, "I feel like an imposter" There's a slight pause before he follows up with, "like I'm the wrong person to lead Kevin, the wrong person to lead this company. Other CEOs must just know what to do in these situations, but I don't."

There it is, the thing that seems to lurk within us all. What if I'm just the wrong person for the job? What if I don't really belong?

As if he could hear my thoughts, Alex continues in a half-mumble, "What if I'm the reason why we fail?"

Being an entrepreneur is really difficult, and failure is constantly nipping at your heels. Feeling like an imposter will get in the way of his ability to move forward and project confidence. "Alex," I say. "First of all, feeling like an imposter is probably the most common feeling for any CEO, whether they're willing to admit it or not. Second, a successful company is a *team* effort. You can't be the only reason it fails any more than you can be the only reason it succeeds."

I give him a second to see if he wants to argue with me, but all I hear are the sounds of the highway. I go on. "Lastly, your awareness of that fear is a strength that many leaders don't have. The fact that you even noticed you were swinging between wanting to save him and fire him is a huge win."

"What do I do with that?" There's still a softness to his voice, but he's coming out of it. I can tell.

There are probably a dozen things I want to say, but in this moment, simplicity is going to be the most helpful. I close my eyes and try to picture what I want him to hear. "Stop trying to control the outcome and focus instead on meeting people where they are."

"What does that mean?"

"You have this idea that you can force Kevin to be better at his job by *willing* it to be, which makes you have to either doubt him or yourself. What if you just met him where he's at and dealt with that instead?"

"So just focus on what he's doing that's not working instead of whether he can do it?"

"Yes! What if we focused more on the outcome and the behavior than we did on the person? Pay attention to the behaviors you want from him and from yourself."

Alex's car has gone silent, and I'm guessing that he's reached his destination. He's quiet for a moment. "This is scary stuff." He offers a short laugh. "I just want this to be easier."

Don't we all? I try to think of something that I can say that will quickly sum up this work for him. "Alex, all I know is that everyone is scared, all the time. We're afraid to connect honestly and openly with another person, so we try to control them. Kevin needs clear feedback on what you want from him, and in order for you to give that, you will need to tell him exactly what you want from him, *which means that you will have to deal with your fear of saying exactly what you want.*"

I hear silence first and then a sigh on the other end of the line.

"How do I do that?"

I lean against the brick wall behind me, recognizing how big this question is.

"Maybe you're already doing it? Just by acknowledging what's happening, I think that you're already ahead of most people. If you can make space for your feelings, then maybe you can make space for Kevin's. I'm not saying that he will be the right person for the job in the long run. That's to be determined. At the least, he will have a chance. The important thing is that you're willing to stay with him."

When we hang up, I'm still thinking about that question: *how do I do that?* How do I deal with the fear?

What I couldn't figure out how to tell him over the phone is how he and all my other clients are teaching me the answer to this every day. It's about leading from a place of authenticity and personal truth. It's about connecting with people as a human being and meeting them as equals. If we do this, we get to be better leaders, teachers, friends and parents. When we take the time to recognize our patterns, see how we impact others, and drop all the ways that we try to defend and protect ourselves from real connection, we become free to communicate with integrity, influence and compassion.

Taming the wolf:

While it's one thing to want perfect work, it's another thing entirely to expect human beings to *be* perfect. In my way of thinking, when we ask others to be perfect for us, we are asking them to make us feel safe. This kind of culture makes it psychologically unsafe for mistakes, and therefore you stunt growth and learning.

One of the elements of perfection is expecting others to read your mind. As Alex realizes this, he is also able to notice how much pressure he is putting on Kevin (and on the organization). Kevin's growth is dependent on understanding what his boss wants from him and *for* him. The clearer you are about what you want, the easier it is to open the channel of communication with your teams.

There's some freedom in recognizing that everyone is scared, pretty much all of the time. Understanding what you're scared of is a way to manage what you bring to the table when you talk to your team. My recommendation here is to look at your assumptions and the fears that drive them (fear of rejection, embarrassment, or failure, for example).

Often the fear shows up as resistance in yourself. So pay attention to that. Uncover your assumptions bring them to the surface. In terms of compassion, remember that your struggles and their struggles are the same. It's just that our insides feel different from what other people's outsides look like.

Everyone is struggling to be heard, be seen and be safe. Have compassion for the human being under you and be clear with them about the expectations you have for them. Don't let your own fears get in the way. Open the channel of communication, and they will not only be grateful, but they will also begin to trust themselves more.

No Time for Shyness

used to teach Homer's *Odyssey* for my Sophomore English classes. One of my favorite moments in that story is about Odysseus' abandoned son, Telemachus. Early in the book, he has to speak to King Nestor to ask for information about his father. As an inexperienced young man, he feels wholly inadequate to the task and says so out loud. Athena chastises him: "Telemachus, no more shyness, this is not the time!" This is not the time to be afraid to be yourself. Here is an invitation from the past that feels as relevant as ever in the present.

What if you could trust your voice more?

I think about Sandeep who felt thwarted by his own inability to clearly communicate his perspective to the other leaders. It can be disorientating to be able to help, and yet feel shut out. I admire his willingness to be curious about what it was that he really wanted them to hear. I also think of Barbara, who was also held back by how people perceived her. She's an example of how powerful a person can be when she understands the power she holds within. In both cases, the clients looked inside themselves for the confidence they needed to lead, in spite of the lack of support from leadership.

I think about Drew and Mateo, both of whom struggled to have influence with their peers and both of whom had to learn to be vulnerable, drop their stories, and be more curious about themselves. Too often I see people get to this point and rather than soften, push harder to do it the way they've always done it. It's difficult to let go of those old habits.

Into the Wolf asks you to embrace the power of your own voice and to imagine that this is the time. This is *your* time. The time for you to drop the habits and patterns that keep you from sharing your whole presence with others. Maybe the only thing that's stopping you is that fear of the unknown.

For many of us, the wolf is guarding the door between the person we are and the person that we know we could become. All we need to do is to step through the uncertainty and claim it. But what a terrifying proposition, to leave behind the behaviors that made us feel as if we were in control. I know.

Every time I'm encouraged to be more open, to communicate with more clarity, and to trust myself more, I recoil. I never feel as though I am fully ready. The work for each of us is to learn how to accept ourselves and the ways that we are being called to change. Have courage and patience.

Once you step into the wolf, all the fear, uncertainty, and self-doubt will melt away. You will discover what's been hidden inside you all this time. Trust that you will be okay.

In bocca al lupo.

(Crepi!) (May it die!)